PSYCHIC DEFENSE STRATEGIES

Protecting Your Energy Field in a World of Magic and Psychic Phenomena

D.R. T STEPHENS

S.D.N Publishing

CONTENTS

THE END

169

GENERAL DISCLAIMER

This book is intended to provide informative and educational material on the subject matter covered. The author(s), publisher, and any affiliated parties make no representations or warranties with respect to the accuracy, applicability, completeness, or suitability of the contents herein and specifically disclaim any implied warranties of merchantability or fitness for a particular purpose.

The information contained in this book is for general information purposes only and is not intended to serve as legal, medical, financial, or any other form of professional advice. Readers should consult with appropriate professionals before making any decisions based on the information provided. Neither the author(s) nor the publisher shall be held responsible or liable for any loss, damage, injury, claim, or otherwise, whether direct or indirect, consequential, or incidental, that may occur as a result of applying or misinterpreting the information in this book.

This book may contain references to third-party websites, products, or services. Such references do not constitute an endorsement or recommendation, and the author(s) and publisher are not responsible for any outcomes related to these third-party references.

In no event shall the author(s), publisher, or any affiliated parties be liable for any direct, indirect, punitive, special, incidental, or other consequential damages arising directly or indirectly from any use of this material, which is provided "as is," and without warranties of any kind, express or implied.

By reading this book, you acknowledge and agree that you assume all risks and responsibilities concerning the applicability and consequences of the information provided. You also agree to indemnify, defend, and hold harmless the author(s), publisher, and any affiliated parties from any and all liabilities, claims, demands, actions, and causes of action whatsoever, whether or not foreseeable, that may arise from using or misusing the information contained in this book.

Although every effort has been made to ensure the accuracy of the information in this book as of the date of publication, the landscape of the subject matter covered is continuously evolving. Therefore, the author(s) and publisher expressly disclaim responsibility for any errors or omissions and reserve the right to update, alter, or revise the content without prior notice.

By continuing to read this book, you agree to be bound by the terms and conditions stated in this disclaimer. If you do not agree with these terms, it is your responsibility to discontinue use of this book immediately.

CHAPTER 1: INTRODUCTION TO PSYCHIC DEFENSE

In an era when interest in esoteric and paranormal phenomena is on the rise, the need for psychic defense has never been more pertinent. As our collective fascination with magic, psychic abilities, and the unseen dimensions of reality gains momentum, so too does the urgency for understanding how to protect oneself energetically. This chapter serves as an introduction to the expansive subject of psychic defense, providing an overview of its importance, the resurgence of interest in magic and psychic phenomena, and how these concepts relate to modern energetic practices.

Why Psychic Defense Matters

Psychic defense is crucial because we exist not just in a physical world but also in a complex interplay of energy fields and psychic spaces. As you navigate through life, you interact continuously with energies—both seen and unseen—that can have a profound impact on your mental, emotional, and even physical well-being. Just as you wouldn't leave your front door open to anyone and anything, you also wouldn't want to leave your energetic field vulnerable to intrusion or influence from external sources.

But this isn't only about warding off negative energies or hostile psychic attacks. Psychic defense also enables you to maintain your own energetic integrity. With the increasing pace and complexity of modern life, there is a lot of psychic "noise" that can create stress, confusion, and emotional disarray. Having a strong psychic defense helps in filtering out this noise, allowing for greater clarity, focus, and peace of mind.

The Contemporary Surge in Interest

We are experiencing a renewed interest in psychic phenomena, magic, and energetic practices. Whether we attribute this to the growth of New Age spirituality, the popularity of witchcraft and the occult, or the more widespread acceptance of Eastern philosophies, the fact remains that many people are actively seeking a deeper, metaphysical understanding of the world.

This surge in interest is not without its dangers. Psychic practices can open up new vistas of experience, offering avenues for personal growth, healing, and insight. However, they can also make one vulnerable to a range of psychic risks, from the minor disturbances caused by "energy vampires" to more deliberate and malicious psychic attacks. As the popularity of psychic and magical practices increases, so too does the likelihood of encountering such risks, making the study and application of psychic defense methods all the more important.

Psychic Defense and Modern Energetic Practices

Psychic defense is inextricably tied to various contemporary practices that deal with energy manipulation and transformation. These include Reiki, chakra balancing, aura cleansing, and the use of crystals, among others. All these practices involve the manipulation or channeling of energy in some form, and thus, they inherently contain the potential for both benefit and risk.

For example, in chakra balancing, the objective is to align and harmonize the seven primary energy centers within the human body. This can lead to profound improvements in both mental and physical health. However, the process of opening up your chakras can also make you susceptible to external energies. Without adequate protection, you may unwittingly absorb negative energies or become the target of an intentional psychic intrusion.

Psychic defense strategies can act as a safeguard, allowing you to engage in these practices while minimizing the associated risks. Whether you're a practitioner of energy work or someone who is simply exploring their psychic sensitivities, understanding how to protect yourself is essential.

Psychic defense is not just a luxury but a necessity, especially in a world that is increasingly open to psychic and magical practices. A strong psychic defense serves as your energetic shield, protecting you from negative influences and allowing you to maintain your energetic integrity. As our collective curiosity in the unseen realms continues to grow, so does the importance of being well-armed against the potential psychic pitfalls that come with it. With a comprehensive understanding of psychic defense, you can explore the mystical dimensions of existence more safely and more profoundly. This book aims to equip you with the knowledge and tools you need to do just that.

CHAPTER 2:
UNDERSTANDING
PSYCHIC PHENOMENA

As we delve into the world of psychic defense, it's essential to first understand the range and scope of psychic phenomena that exist. A foundational understanding will help us better recognize the advantages and the risks these phenomena pose. This chapter aims to clarify the different types of psychic phenomena, including clairvoyance, telepathy, and remote viewing, among others, and discuss their implications for personal safety and well-being.

Types of Psychic Phenomena

- **Clairvoyance**: This is perhaps one of the most well-known psychic abilities, often referred to as 'clear seeing.' Individuals with clairvoyance claim to perceive events, objects, or people that are not within their standard range of vision, often transcending time and space.

- **Telepathy**: This involves the direct transmission of thoughts between individuals, bypassing the conventional senses. While the scientific community remains skeptical, numerous anecdotal accounts suggest that telepathic communication can occur spontaneously or be developed through specific practices.

- **Remote Viewing**: Unlike clairvoyance, remote viewing is often described as a more disciplined practice. It involves seeing a distant or unseen target using extrasensory perception (ESP). Some government programs have even explored the military applications of remote viewing.

- **Empathy**: Often confused with telepathy, psychic empathy involves sensing the emotions and feelings of others. This can be both a gift and a burden, as absorbing too much from others can lead to emotional exhaustion.

- **Precognition and Retrocognition**: These phenomena involve knowledge of future events (precognition) or past events (retrocognition) that cannot be explained by ordinary means. While controversial, these phenomena persist in cultural narratives and personal testimonies.

- **Psychokinesis**: This involves the ability to manipulate physical objects using the power of the mind alone. Reports range from bending spoons to influencing the roll of dice.

- **Mediumship**: This involves communication with non-physical entities, often said to be spirits of the deceased. The medium acts as a bridge between the physical and spiritual worlds.

Benefits and Risks

Understanding psychic phenomena is not just about cataloging interesting or mysterious abilities; it's also about recognizing the implications these have for individuals and communities. On the positive side, psychic phenomena can:

1. Enhance Self-Awareness: Understanding your psychic capabilities can lead to a deeper sense of self and life purpose.

2. Facilitate Healing: Abilities like psychic empathy can be used to identify and heal emotional or physical wounds, whether in oneself or others.

3. Guide Decision-Making: Intuitive abilities, if properly honed, can serve as an internal guidance system.

However, these abilities also come with inherent risks:

1. Exploitation: Psychic abilities can be used to manipulate or deceive individuals, either for personal gain or to cause harm.

2. Emotional Drain: Abilities like empathy can lead to emotional exhaustion, especially when exposed to negative environments or individuals.

3. Misinformation: Not all psychic information is accurate or useful. Mistaking psychic phenomena for incontrovertible fact can lead to poor decisions and outcomes.

Psychic Phenomena and Defense

Understanding these phenomena is crucial for psychic defense. Knowing the type of psychic phenomena you're experiencing can help you better defend against them. For example, if you're particularly empathic, you'll need different defense mechanisms than someone who is more clairvoyant. Additionally, understanding these phenomena can also help you distinguish between what might be a genuine psychic attack and what could be a natural manifestation of your abilities or even psychological conditions, which we'll explore in later chapters.

Understanding the range of psychic phenomena is foundational for anyone interested in or concerned with psychic defense. These phenomena, from clairvoyance to telepathy to psychokinesis, offer both incredible potential and inherent risks. Recognizing the specific types of phenomena can guide you in adopting the appropriate defense mechanisms, thereby enhancing your psychic well-being and general safety. As we proceed, this understanding will serve as a building block for more advanced defense strategies, including discerning genuine psychic phenomena from psychological conditions and employing more nuanced protection mechanisms.

CHAPTER 3:
THE NATURE OF
ENERGY FIELDS

In the sphere of psychic phenomena and defense, the concept of energy fields or auras plays a pivotal role. This chapter delves into the nature of these invisible fields that are believed to surround living beings, examining their characteristics, structures, and functions. We will explore how understanding energy fields can serve as an essential building block in effective psychic defense strategies.

The Basic Structure of Energy Fields

Energy fields, often colloquially referred to as "auras," are considered the intangible, multi-dimensional halos that encompass physical bodies. The idea is that these fields interact continuously with both internal and external energies. They act as a sort of filter and protective shield, allowing positive energy to enter while attempting to repel negative energies.

Various esoteric systems break down the aura into multiple layers, each with its distinct function. Common layers discussed in different traditions include:

- The Etheric Layer: This is the closest layer to the physical body and is often considered a blueprint of the physical form. It is said to govern physical sensations and comfort.

- The Emotional Layer: Situated beyond the Etheric, this layer supposedly reflects emotional states and psychological mood.

- The Mental Layer: This deals with thoughts, mental processes, and intellectual reasoning.

- The Spiritual Layer: The outermost layer is believed to connect individuals with higher consciousness and divine forces.

It is worth noting that these layers are not universally agreed upon, and different systems might describe the aura in various ways. However, the core idea remains: these layers interact and influence each other, playing a role in both psychic phenomena and defense.

Functions and Interactions

Energy fields are not just static, decorative glows; they are dynamic and constantly shifting based on several factors. These factors may include an individual's emotional state, physical health, and even the environment they are in. The energy field is thought to both emit and absorb energy, and this is where its interaction with psychic phenomena becomes crucial.

For example, when someone is emotionally distressed, it is thought that their energy field might become disorganized or 'leaky,' making them more susceptible to external psychic influences. On the flip side, someone with a strong, well-organized energy field might naturally repel negative energies. This dynamic nature of energy fields forms the foundation for psychic defense techniques such as grounding and shielding, which aim to reinforce the aura.

Moreover, energy fields can also interact with each other. In group settings or close relationships, individual energy fields may blend, creating a collective energy dynamic. This collective field can be either harmonious or dissonant based on the compatibility of individual auras and intentions. Psychic defense techniques often aim to maintain the integrity of one's energy field when entering collective settings.

Energy Fields and Psychic Defense

Understanding your energy field is like understanding the boundaries of your psychic 'territory.' Fortifying this territory is the essence of psychic defense. The idea is to keep your energy field strong, harmonious, and clear, which in turn helps in repelling unwanted psychic or energetic intrusions. Techniques to cleanse, balance, and protect the energy field form the bedrock of psychic defense, which will be elaborated upon in subsequent chapters.

By paying attention to how you feel in different environments and situations, you can get a sense of the quality and stability of your energy field. Some people even resort to energy field 'readings' from specialized practitioners to gain insights into the state of their auras. Regardless of your approach, acknowledging and respecting your energy field can offer a potent line of defense against psychic vulnerabilities.

Energy fields, commonly known as auras, serve as an intrinsic component in the realm of psychic phenomena and defense. These dynamic, multi-layered fields are believed to filter and interact with different forms of energy, playing a critical role in psychic wellbeing. The characteristics and interactions of energy fields form the basis for multiple psychic defense strategies aimed at fortifying these invisible boundaries. A deeper understanding of your energy field can serve as an invaluable tool in your arsenal for psychic protection.

CHAPTER 4:
HISTORICAL
BACKGROUND OF
PSYCHIC DEFENSE

The concept of psychic defense isn't a new one, shaped by modern sensibilities or discoveries. Rather, it has ancient roots that stretch across diverse cultures and epochs. This chapter aims to excavate the historical bedrock of psychic defense methods to offer a nuanced understanding of its evolution over time. The ancestral wisdom embedded in these historical approaches is often surprisingly relevant to contemporary practices.

Ancient Civilizations and Psychic Defense

The earliest records of psychic defense mechanisms can be traced back to civilizations such as Mesopotamia, Egypt, and ancient China. While the terminologies differed, the fundamental idea remained constant: an unseen energy or force could influence human lives, either for good or ill.

In Mesopotamia, cuneiform tablets describe various rituals and spells aimed at warding off malevolent spirits. The Egyptians, meanwhile, were known for their intricate talismans like the "Eye of Horus," believed to offer protection against evil forces. Pharaohs and high priests often employed complex rituals to protect their energy fields. Ancient Chinese traditions also included similar concepts, particularly within Taoism. Techniques like Qigong were not only exercises for physical health but were also understood to balance the Chi (Qi), the vital energy flowing within and around a person, providing a form of psychic defense.

Middle Ages to Renaissance: Alchemy, Hermeticism, and Beyond

Fast forward to medieval Europe, and we find that the convergence of religion, mysticism, and the early stirrings of science led to intricate systems of psychic defense. Alchemy, which many today misunderstand as mere proto-chemistry, was deeply spiritual. The alchemical process aimed not just to transform base metals into gold, but also to achieve spiritual purification. This purification acted as a shield against negative psychic energies.

During the Renaissance, the revival of Neoplatonism and

Hermeticism led to a more structured formulation of psychic defense. The writings attributed to Hermes Trismegistus laid out philosophies and rituals aimed at aligning oneself with the cosmic order, thereby offering protection against psychic discord. The grimoires of the time, such as the "Key of Solomon," also contained a multitude of spells and protective sigils designed to guard against psychic attacks.

Indigenous Cultures and Shamanic Practices

Away from the well-documented corridors of "Western" history, indigenous cultures around the world have developed their unique systems of psychic defense. These are often shamanic in nature and rooted deeply in the land and local spirituality. Native American, African, and Siberian shamans, among others, performed intricate rituals to cleanse individuals and places from malicious energies. Totems, amulets, and the use of sacred plants like sage in smudging ceremonies have all been employed as shields against negative psychic influences.

Whether it's the Aboriginal Dreamtime stories that explain the energetic ties between humans and the Earth, or the Andean cosmology that integrates the concept of "ayni" (sacred reciprocity) as a form of spiritual balance and defense, indigenous methods frequently emphasize living in harmony with the environment as a way of natural psychic defense.

From the dawn of civilization to modern times, the idea of psychic defense has transcended cultural and geographical boundaries. Though the methods may vary, the underpinning belief systems highlight the human need for safeguarding the unseen, vital aspects of our existence. As we navigate the complexities of our contemporary lives, often fraught with their own types of psychic challenges, we may find that these age-old strategies offer not just historical insights but also practical applications. Their enduring presence across millennia testifies to their intrinsic value, and studying them can empower us to adapt and adopt these time-tested methods for our own psychic well-being.

CHAPTER 5: RECOGNIZING PSYCHIC ATTACKS

The ability to recognize a psychic attack is a cornerstone of effective psychic defense. Without accurate identification, it becomes nearly impossible to deploy countermeasures or safeguard one's energy effectively. This chapter will delve into the symptoms and signs often associated with psychic attacks, and importantly, differentiate between genuine psychic phenomena and psychological conditions.

Symptoms and Signs of a Psychic Attack

Individuals who experience psychic attacks often describe a range of symptoms that are physical, emotional, and mental in nature. The following are some common manifestations:

- **Physical Discomfort**: Sudden, unexplained headaches, dizziness, or a feeling of heaviness may occur. Some also report episodes of nausea or a sense of being drained of energy.

- **Emotional Imbalance**: Frequent mood swings, feelings of depression, or heightened anxiety can signal a psychic attack. One may also experience an inexplicable sense of dread or fear.

- **Mental Fog**: The person may face difficulty in concentrating, experience memory lapses, or have clouded judgement. A sustained attack can even lead to obsessive thoughts or nightmares.

These signs are not definitive proof of a psychic attack but should serve as red flags urging one to investigate further. The more of these symptoms one experiences in a concentrated timeframe, particularly in a setting rich in psychic energy or activities, the higher the likelihood of experiencing a psychic attack.

Differentiating Psychic Phenomena from Psychological Conditions

The symptoms mentioned are not exclusive to psychic attacks and can mimic other conditions such as psychological stress, medical disorders, or even common fatigue. Therefore, it is essential to rule out other plausible explanations. Here are some considerations:

- **Timing and Context**: Did these symptoms appear suddenly, especially after a specific event, ritual, or after interacting with a particular person known for

D.R. TSTEPHENS

psychic activities? If so, there's a greater chance of it being a psychic attack.

- **Elimination of Other Causes**: Before jumping to conclusions, it's important to consult with healthcare providers to rule out any underlying medical or psychological conditions that could be causing these symptoms.
- **Psychic Sensitivity**: Individuals with heightened psychic sensitivity are generally more attuned to changes in psychic energy. If you belong to this category, your intuition could serve as an additional gauge.

Common Misconceptions and Pitfalls

Misdiagnosis or mistaking other issues for psychic attacks is not uncommon. Sometimes, what is perceived as an attack might just be an accumulation of negative energy from one's surroundings, which can be cleared through grounding or cleansing techniques.

Another pitfall is over-attributing all negative life events to psychic attacks, which can create a mindset of constant vulnerability and fear, thereby weakening one's natural psychic defenses. Developing a discerning approach to recognizing psychic attacks can empower individuals to respond appropriately without being caught in a spiral of unnecessary anxiety and defensive measures.

Recognizing the signs of a psychic attack is a critical first step in defending one's energy field. While physical, emotional, and mental symptoms can serve as indicators, it's essential to exercise discernment in differentiating these from other medical or psychological conditions. Being cautious about pitfalls like over-attribution is also crucial. Accurate recognition

22

allows for the timely implementation of psychic defense mechanisms, serving as a robust shield against energetic disruptions.

CHAPTER 6: SOURCES OF PSYCHIC ATTACKS

Understanding the origins and sources of psychic attacks is crucial for effective psychic defense. Knowledge of what can trigger an attack or where it may come from allows you to prepare, shield, and even preemptively neutralize threats to your energy field. This chapter delves into various sources that can instigate psychic attacks, ranging from intentional actions by practitioners to unintentional negative energy and environmental factors.

Intentional Attacks from Practitioners

One of the most obvious and direct sources of psychic attacks comes from individuals proficient in psychic or magical practices. Whether motivated by jealousy, revenge, or a desire for power, these individuals may intentionally send negative energies your way. The methods employed can vary widely— from curses and hexes to direct psychic intrusion into your energy field. What makes these attacks especially challenging to deal with is the skill level of the practitioner involved. A skilled practitioner may use intricate rituals or spells that are hard to trace or counteract. However, it's important to remember that ethical practitioners of psychic or magical arts generally adhere to a code that prohibits unwarranted attacks on others, subscribing to the principle of "do no harm."

Unintentional Negative Energy

Not all psychic attacks are intentional. You can also be affected by unintentional negative energy sent your way. This could come from people who harbor strong negative emotions towards you but have no idea how their energy can impact others. For example, someone going through a particularly challenging time may emanate negative energy that can affect those around them. Alternatively, a person who intensely dislikes you may unintentionally send harmful energies your way, especially during emotionally charged confrontations. The person emanating this energy may be completely unaware of their influence, making it less malicious but not necessarily less damaging.

Environmental Factors

A less obvious but equally potent source of psychic attacks can be your environment. Geopathic stress, for instance, can emanate from certain natural features of the Earth, such as underground water streams or specific mineral concentrations, which can interfere with your energy field. Built environments are also relevant; think of a room where an argument took place, the negative energy from that event can linger and affect subsequent occupants. Cultural or collective energy can also serve as a source. In areas with a history of trauma, such as war zones or places of severe social injustice, the accumulated energy can pose a psychic threat to individuals who are sensitive to such energies.

These environmental factors can also amplify existing vulnerabilities in your psychic defenses. For instance, spending extended periods in a toxic workplace can weaken your energy field, making you more susceptible to psychic intrusions from other sources. Similarly, collective psychic phenomena like mass hysteria can emanate from a particular environment and affect multiple individuals within that space.

Understanding the possible sources of psychic attacks enables you to tailor your defense mechanisms more effectively. While intentional attacks from skilled practitioners may require specialized countermeasures, unintentional sources and environmental factors often require a more nuanced approach, such as cleansing the space or using shielding techniques that protect against a broader spectrum of energies. Recognizing the varied nature of these sources also facilitates a more compassionate approach to psychic defense, allowing for remedies that not only protect you but can also heal or neutralize the source itself when possible.

Gaining a multifaceted understanding of where psychic attacks may originate equips you with the foundational knowledge to preemptively protect your energy field. Armed with this information, you can now navigate your physical and psychic environment with heightened awareness, empowered to neutralize threats and maintain your energetic equilibrium.

CHAPTER 7: BASIC PSYCHIC DEFENSE MECHANISMS

The preceding chapters have laid the groundwork for understanding what psychic defense is, why it's crucial in the modern world, and what forms psychic attacks can take. With that understanding in place, this chapter will focus on introducing you to some fundamental techniques for psychic defense, particularly grounding and shielding. These techniques serve as the backbone for any psychic defense strategy, offering immediate measures for protection and acting as a starting point for more advanced practices.

Grounding Techniques

Grounding refers to the act of energetically anchoring oneself to the Earth or another stabilizing force. This practice helps you to establish a firm foundation from which to operate, making you less susceptible to external influences. Grounding serves both as a defensive mechanism against psychic attacks and a way to rejuvenate and balance your energy field.

1. **Physical Grounding**: One of the most straightforward grounding techniques is physical grounding. It involves literally making contact with the ground, usually by walking barefoot on soil, grass, or sand. The Earth possesses its own magnetic field and electrical charge, which can stabilize and harmonize your energy.

2. **Visual Grounding**: This technique is often performed through guided visualization. One common practice is to imagine roots growing from the soles of your feet into the Earth. These roots go deep into the ground, anchoring you firmly. As you breathe in, imagine absorbing the Earth's energy, and as you breathe out, visualize releasing any negativity.

3. **Breathing and Centering**: Breathwork can also serve as grounding when you focus on your breath and use it to center your thoughts. Inhaling deeply through the nose, holding the breath briefly, and exhaling through the mouth can act as a quick way to center and ground yourself.

Shielding Techniques

While grounding helps to stabilize your energy, shielding techniques are employed to create a protective barrier around you. Think of it like building an energetic wall or armor that filters out negative energies and psychic intrusions.

1. **White Light Shield**: One of the most popular methods involves envisioning a white light emanating from your heart or crown chakra, expanding until it encircles your entire body in a protective sphere. The light serves as a barrier that only allows positive energy to enter.

2. **Mirror Shield**: Another shielding technique employs the power of reflection. Here, you visualize a shield made of mirrors facing outward around you. The mirrors reflect any negative energy or psychic attack back to its source.

3. **Elemental Shields**: Some individuals resonate more with natural elements like fire, water, earth, or air. In such cases, you can create a shield using the imagery of these elements. For instance, envisioning a wall of fire or a swirling vortex of water around you can serve as a protective shield.

Combining Grounding and Shielding

For optimal results, grounding and shielding can be used in conjunction. Grounding yourself first ensures that your energy is stabilized and centered, making your shields more robust and effective. After grounding, you can proceed to erect your chosen shield, reinforcing it as needed.

When performed consistently, these basic techniques create a solid foundation for psychic defense. They are adaptable to various situations, whether you find yourself in a challenging emotional environment, facing a direct psychic attack, or simply navigating the stresses of everyday life. They are not just reactive measures for defense but also proactive steps that contribute to psychic hygiene, helping to maintain a balanced and fortified energy field.

Grounding and shielding are cornerstone techniques in the practice of psychic defense. Grounding anchors you to a stable energy source like the Earth, making you less susceptible to negative influences. Shielding, on the other hand, provides an active defense by creating an energetic barrier around you. Together, these fundamental practices offer a robust defense against psychic intrusions, providing a strong foundation upon which more advanced techniques can be built. Given their versatility and effectiveness, they are essential tools in the psychic defense toolkit for both novices and seasoned practitioners alike.

CHAPTER 8:
ADVANCED
PSYCHIC DEFENSE
TECHNIQUES

After exploring basic methods for psychic defense, such as grounding and shielding, it becomes necessary to delve into more advanced techniques. These advanced methods are generally designed for those who have honed their psychic abilities, and are familiar with concepts and practices related to energy work. This chapter elucidates three complex but effective techniques: mirror shields, psychic "firewalls," and invoking spiritual allies.

Mirror Shields

Mirror shields operate on the principle of reflection. The primary aim is to reflect negative energies, thoughts, or psychic attacks back to their source. The process of creating a mirror shield involves advanced visualization techniques. Unlike basic shields that absorb or block incoming energies, mirror shields bounce these energies back.

To construct a mirror shield, one must first be well-practiced in grounding and creating basic shields. Begin with a meditative state and visualize a sphere of protective energy around yourself, just as you would with a basic shield. Once this sphere is complete, imagine it turning into a mirror facing outward. Envision the surface becoming increasingly reflective, fortified by your intent to protect yourself.

It is crucial to hold no malice while setting up a mirror shield. The purpose isn't to harm anyone but simply to reflect back any negative energy. This maintains an ethical boundary and ensures that you don't inadvertently send out negative energy yourself.

Psychic Firewalls

Drawing an analogy from computer technology, a psychic firewall acts as an advanced filtering system for your energy field. The idea is to permit beneficial energies while automatically blocking or transforming harmful ones. Psychic firewalls are often complex constructs imbued with specific "if-then" conditions programmed through intent and visualization.

For instance, you can program your psychic firewall to allow only energies that are beneficial to you while converting negative energies into neutral or positive forms. The more specific you can be in your "programming," the more effective the firewall. Some practitioners even integrate symbols, words, or mantras into their firewalls for added power.

To set up a psychic firewall, you must be proficient in meditation and focused intent. Start by entering a meditative state and establish a basic energy shield. Then, visualize complex layers forming over the shield, with each layer designated to filter specific types of energy. Infuse these layers with your specific intentions, ensuring that your "programming" is clear and precise.

Invoking Spiritual Allies

Enlisting the help of spiritual allies like guardian angels, spirit guides, or ancestral spirits can significantly enhance your psychic defense. This is often considered one of the most potent forms of protection but also demands a high level of spiritual connection and ethical consideration.

Begin by entering a deeply meditative or trance-like state, grounding yourself thoroughly. Call upon your spiritual ally clearly and respectfully, asking for their assistance in fortifying your psychic defenses. Always remember to express gratitude and offer something in return, whether it's an energetic offering or a promise to do good deeds.

Maintaining a relationship with your spiritual allies is key; this is not a one-time transaction but a mutual relationship. Regularly communicate with them, honoring them in your daily life or through specific rituals to strengthen your spiritual bonds and thus, your psychic defenses.

Advanced psychic defense techniques offer more robust forms

of protection, especially for those who are well-practiced in psychic and energetic work. Mirror shields act as reflectors of negative energies, psychic firewalls serve as advanced filters, and invoking spiritual allies provides potent protection through spiritual partnerships. These methods often require a higher degree of skill, focus, and ethical consideration but offer effective ways to safeguard your energetic well-being. As you continue on your journey of psychic self-defense, these advanced techniques can prove invaluable tools in your arsenal.

CHAPTER 9: PSYCHIC SELF-CARE

After diving into the complexities of psychic defense, from recognizing psychic attacks to advanced protective mechanisms, we arrive at the subject of psychic self-care. This chapter emphasizes the importance of taking a holistic approach to fortify your psychic defenses. The concept here is akin to preventive medicine in healthcare: rather than solely focusing on defending against attacks or negative energies, we nurture a lifestyle that inherently strengthens our psychic resilience. In essence, a well-maintained energy field can be your best defense.

The Symbiosis of Physical and Psychic Well-Being

It's a fallacy to consider psychic well-being as entirely separate from physical or emotional health. The three are inextricably linked. Physical ailments can often manifest due to imbalances or vulnerabilities in one's energy field. Conversely, a well-balanced energy field can contribute to a healthier body and mind.

Exercise and Movement

Engaging in regular physical activity has clear physiological benefits, but it's also a potent way to stimulate and balance the body's energy centers or chakras. The rhythmic movements in exercises such as running, swimming, or even yoga can help in loosening any energy blockages and promote a smoother flow of energy throughout the body.

Nutrition and Hydration

The food we consume serves not just as physical fuel but as sustenance for our energy field. Diets rich in processed foods, sugars, and unhealthy fats can generate a form of psychic "sludge" that hampers the energy field. On the other hand, foods that are organic, fresh, and rich in essential nutrients can enhance the vibrancy of one's aura. Similarly, hydration plays a crucial role. Just as water serves to cleanse the physical body, it assists in the energetic cleansing of the energy field.

Mindfulness and Emotional Regulation

The state of your mind has a direct impact on your energy

field. Persistent negative thoughts or emotional turmoil can introduce vulnerabilities in your psychic defenses.

Mindfulness and Meditation

Mindfulness practices and meditation serve as tools for becoming aware of your thought patterns, emotional states, and, by extension, the state of your energy field. By bringing attention to the present moment, you can identify and rectify any disruptive elements within your energy field before they escalate into bigger issues.

Emotional Regulation Techniques

Psychic self-care involves more than just awareness; it requires active management of your emotional state. Techniques like emotional freedom techniques (EFT), also known as tapping, can be quite effective. EFT involves tapping on specific points on the body while vocalizing positive affirmations or confronting negative emotions, effectively acting as a form of acupressure for the emotions and, by extension, the energy field.

Spirituality and Connection

Spirituality here does not necessarily pertain to religious practices (though it can), but to the understanding that you are part of a broader universe and connected to a higher form of energy. This realization can be profoundly comforting and strengthening for your energy field.

Rituals and Sacred Spaces

Creating a sacred space for prayer, meditation, or even contemplation can fortify your psychic defenses. The very act of designating a space as 'sacred' elevates its energetic quality. Rituals, whether they are complex ceremonies or simple routines like lighting a candle before meditation, add layers of intent that can buttress your energy field.

Connection to Nature

Spending time in natural settings, such as forests, beaches, or mountains, can serve as a form of spiritual nourishment. These environments are rich in positive energy, which can cleanse and recharge your energy field.

Psychic self-care is not an isolated practice but a lifestyle choice that intersects with physical, emotional, and spiritual well-being. It serves as both a preventive and augmentative strategy for psychic defense. By fostering a harmonious energy field through holistic practices that range from diet and exercise to emotional regulation and spiritual connectivity, you create an environment where negative energies find it difficult to take hold. In doing so, you build a robust first line of defense that complements more targeted psychic defense techniques.

CHAPTER 10: THE ETHICS OF PSYCHIC DEFENSE

The practice of psychic defense is imbued with a variety of ethical considerations that often go unexplored in the excitement of mastering new techniques. While the primary goal is self-preservation and the safeguarding of one's energetic well-being, the means to achieve that end can sometimes tread into morally ambiguous territories. This chapter delves into these ethical quandaries, tackling topics like the border between defense and aggression, the nuances of intent, and the imperative of respecting others' free will.

The Thin Line between Defense and Attack

In the metaphysical realm, the distinction between defensive and offensive maneuvers can often become blurred. For instance, one could argue that a psychic "firewall" not only blocks incoming negative energies but also potentially rebounds them back to the sender. While the motive might be self-protection, the action could have repercussions that may cause harm to another being, even if they had malicious intentions initially. Consequently, it becomes essential to scrutinize the range of defensive methods available and consider their ethical implications. Are you merely deflecting a psychic attack, or are you pushing back with an energy that could harm another? This line can be thin, and walking it requires not just skill but also moral discernment.

The Ethics of Intent

The realm of psychic phenomena is significantly influenced by the principle of intent. Your mental and emotional state, your motives, and your awareness play a considerable role in the ethical dimensions of psychic defense. Engaging in defensive practices with a heart filled with vengeance or malice can inadvertently transform a protective act into an aggressive one. It's not just the technique employed but the energy and thought behind it that determines its ethical standing.

Moreover, intent becomes particularly complex when dealing with 'unintentional' psychic attackers. These are individuals who may not be consciously aware that their energy is invasive or harmful. How does one ethically manage defenses against such individuals? The key is to focus on neutralizing the effect rather than retaliating against the person. For instance, you might employ a shielding technique that dissipates negative energy without sending it back to the origin, thereby neutralizing the harm without causing additional suffering.

Respecting Free Will and Autonomy

In metaphysical and spiritual paradigms, the respect for free will is a cornerstone ethical principle. Even in a defensive posture, one must take care not to overpower or manipulate another's energetic field without consent. Imagine a scenario where someone believes they are 'healing' another by sending positive energy or modifying their aura without explicit permission. Although well-intended, this action can be seen as a violation of the other person's spiritual autonomy. The ethics of psychic defense include the need for informed consent when your defensive actions will interact with another's energy field in a substantial way.

The notion of free will also extends to the spirits and entities one might call upon for protection or assistance. Invoking spiritual allies should be conducted with the utmost respect and ideally, an established relationship between the practitioner and the spiritual entity. The indiscriminate summoning of spiritual forces not only risks ineffectiveness but could also be considered disrespectful or manipulative, thereby contravening ethical norms.

Ethics in psychic defense constitute a nuanced and often complex area that demands thoughtful consideration. It is not merely a checklist but a philosophical framework that ought to guide your practices. The ethical practitioner will be mindful of the fine line between defense and aggression, committed to clarity of intent, and vigilant in respecting the free will of others, whether in the physical or spiritual realms. Given that actions in the metaphysical realm can have far-reaching consequences, perhaps even more than in the physical world, adhering to ethical principles isn't just a matter of moral uprightness. It's crucial for maintaining the balance and integrity of the intricate web of energies that we navigate daily. Therefore, as you advance in your practice of psychic defense, continually reflect on the ethical dimensions of your actions to ensure that your protective strategies honor both yourself and the interconnected web of existence in which you partake.

CHAPTER 11:
RITUALS AND TOOLS
FOR DEFENSE

As we have discussed in previous chapters, psychic defense involves a multi-pronged approach ranging from understanding energy fields to advanced psychic techniques. In this chapter, we will explore a specific subset of psychic defense strategies that involve rituals, talismans, and other physical tools. These objects and actions can serve as powerful aids in both warding off negative energies and reinforcing your psychic barriers.

Rituals for Psychic Defense

Rituals, being structured activities imbued with intent, are capable of affecting our psychic energies. Here are some commonly used rituals for psychic defense:

1. **Smudging**: This involves burning herbs such as sage, cedar, or sweetgrass to cleanse a space or aura. The smoke is believed to carry away negative energy.

2. **Salt Baths**: Bathing in a mix of water and salt, particularly Himalayan or Epsom salt, is often recommended to cleanse the aura.

3. **Candle Rituals**: Lighting a candle while focusing on a specific intention, such as protection or healing, can be a potent form of ritual magic. Often, the color of the candle is chosen to correspond with the intention (e.g., black for banishing negativity, white for purity and protection).

4. **Chanting and Mantras**: Vocalizing specific words or phrases can serve to align your energy and invoke protection. The choice of words can be from traditional spiritual practices or something personal that holds meaning for you.

The efficacy of these rituals can be attributed to a variety of factors, including the power of concentrated intention, the symbolism inherent in the actions, and the energetic properties of the materials used.

Talismans and Physical Tools

Physical objects can also act as potent tools for psychic defense. Here's how:

1. **Amulets and Talismans**: These are objects imbued with specific energies or inscriptions to protect the

wearer. The object can range from a traditional symbol, like a pentagram, to something more personal, like a locket with a meaningful photograph.

2. **Sacred Texts**: Carrying or reciting from spiritual or religious texts can offer protection for believers. For example, some people find comfort and protection in reciting verses from the Bible, Quran, or other religious scriptures.

3. **Metals and Stones**: Certain metals, like copper and iron, and stones, like black tourmaline and obsidian, are believed to have properties that ward off negative energies.

These physical objects often serve as both a mental focus point and an energetic filter. The act of carrying them can also serve as a form of ritual.

Crafting Your Own Tools and Rituals

Creating your own psychic defense tools and rituals allows for a highly personalized approach. A self-crafted talisman, imbued with your own energy and intention, can be more effective than a store-bought item. Similarly, creating your own ritual gives you the freedom to incorporate elements that have personal significance, thereby increasing the ritual's effectiveness.

Here's a simplified guide to crafting your own tools and rituals:

1. **Set a Clear Intention**: Know precisely what you wish to achieve. Is it general protection, or is it defense against a specific type of energy?

2. **Choose Your Materials Carefully**: If crafting a talisman, decide on a material that resonates with you and your intention.

3. **Imbue with Energy**: Whether it's a ritual or a physical

object, it needs to be charged with your energy and intent. This can be done through meditation, chanting, or even simply holding the object and focusing your energy upon it.

4. **Regular Upkeep**: Periodically recharge your tools and revise your rituals to ensure they are up-to-date and aligned with your current needs.

Rituals and tools offer a tactile and focused approach to psychic defense, serving as both a psychological aid and an energetic safeguard. Whether you opt for traditional methods or craft your own, the critical factor is the intention and focus you bring into the process. These practices serve to amplify your inherent psychic defense mechanisms, making them a valuable addition to your psychic defense repertoire.

CHAPTER 12:
CRYSTALS FOR
PSYCHIC DEFENSE

The integration of crystals into psychic defense strategies is a topic that has captivated both practitioners and novices alike. Crystals, with their unique energetic vibrations and intricate molecular structures, are believed to have the capacity to interact with the human energy field in a way that can offer protection, clarity, and healing. While the scientific community remains skeptical about the metaphysical properties of crystals, a large number of people find them to be effective tools for various purposes, including psychic defense. In this chapter, we will delve into the roles that different types of crystals can play in psychic protection, how to use them, and the conceptual frameworks that support their usage.

Types of Crystals and Their Protective Qualities

Different crystals possess varying properties that can be tailored to meet specific needs in psychic defense. Here are some commonly used crystals for this purpose:

- **Black Tourmaline**: Often touted as the "shield stone," black tourmaline is renowned for its ability to repel negative energies and protect against psychic attacks.

- **Amethyst**: Known for its calming properties, amethyst is considered effective in warding off emotional and psychic stress. It is also believed to create a protective shield of light around the user.

- **Clear Quartz**: This crystal is considered a universal stone that can amplify any energy or intention, including protective ones. It can also cleanse and align the chakras, making it easier to maintain a healthy energy field.

- **Obsidian**: A grounding stone that can also act as a mirror, reflecting negative energies back to their source.

- **Smoky Quartz**: Also a grounding stone, smoky quartz is believed to neutralize negative energy and protect against electromagnetic smog.

- **Lapis Lazuli**: This stone is thought to boost the immune system and promote psychic clarity, enabling one to discern the true nature of any psychic interaction and protect oneself accordingly.

How to Use Crystals for Psychic Defense

There are several ways to incorporate crystals into your psychic defense routine:

1. **Wearing Them**: Crystals can be worn as jewelry such as necklaces, bracelets, or earrings. This keeps them close to your body and allows for continuous interaction with your energy field.

2. **Placing Them**: Crystals can be placed strategically in living spaces. For instance, black tourmaline can be placed near the entrance of your home to ward off negative energy.

3. **Meditation and Visualization**: During meditation, you can hold a crystal and visualize its energy enveloping you, forming a protective shield.

4. **Crystal Grids**: For more elaborate psychic defense, a crystal grid can be created using multiple stones. The grid serves to synergize the energies of the individual crystals, creating a powerful protective field.

5. **Elixirs**: Some practitioners use crystal-infused water as an elixir for psychic protection, though this method requires caution. Not all crystals are safe to be ingested or even to come into contact with water, so consult reliable references or experts when considering this approach.

Conceptual Frameworks and Criticisms

The use of crystals in psychic defense is often justified through various conceptual frameworks, such as the vibrational energy model, which posits that the unique molecular arrangement of each crystal corresponds to specific energetic frequencies that can interact with human energy fields. Another theory is the color spectrum model, which suggests that the color of the crystal correlates with different chakras and can therefore be used to balance and protect them.

However, it's essential to note that these frameworks lack robust scientific backing. Many scientists and skeptics argue that any perceived benefits from using crystals for psychic defense are placebo effects. Therefore, while many people swear by the effectiveness of crystals, their usage should be supplementary to other more established psychic defense mechanisms unless proven otherwise.

Crystals offer a rich tapestry of options for those looking to augment their psychic defense strategies. With a variety of types to choose from, each with their own unique protective properties, crystals can be a versatile addition to any psychic defense toolkit. However, the effectiveness of these stones is still a subject of debate, and they should be used as a supplement to other psychic defense techniques. Regardless of the skepticism surrounding their use, the enduring popularity of crystals in metaphysical practices suggests that many find them to be useful, meaningful tools in their quest for psychic well-being.

CHAPTER 13:
DEFENSIVE MAGIC
AND SPELLWORK

In the realm of psychic defense, there are numerous tools and techniques at your disposal, each offering its own advantages and intricacies. While previous chapters delved into the utility of crystals, talismans, and ritualistic practices, this chapter aims to discuss defensive magic and spellwork. Magic, in this context, is not the sleight of hand performed by stage magicians, but rather the focused manipulation of energies and forces through willpower, symbols, and rituals to effect change. Spellwork is the act of conducting these magical operations. The premise here is that, like physical laws, there are metaphysical laws which can be harnessed and directed for specific outcomes, including psychic defense.

Principles of Defensive Magic

Defensive magic operates on a few fundamental principles. First is the principle of "Like Attracts Like," commonly known in magical practices as the Law of Attraction. For example, if you create a magical symbol or "sigil" for protection and imbue it with your focused intention, it is believed to attract protective energies. The second principle is the "Law of Contagion," which suggests that objects or symbols that have been in contact with each other have an enduring magical connection. A lock of hair or personal item can therefore be used in spellwork to represent the person it belongs to. These principles aren't just esoteric notions; they are rooted in a combination of historical belief systems, folk practices, and modern interpretations.

Types of Defensive Spells

1. **Protection Spells**: The most straightforward category, these spells aim to create a barrier between you and psychic attacks or negative energies. Common elements include salt, sage, and symbols of protection like pentagrams or runic characters.

2. **Banishing Spells**: These are more proactive and aim to repel negative forces or entities. They may employ elements like fiery herbs, pointed symbols, and strong verbal commands.

3. **Binding Spells**: These spells don't repel or protect; instead, they restrain. Binding spells lock down a threat by symbolically tying it up, often through the use of cords, images, or physical representations like

dolls.

Each type of spell generally involves a combination of spoken words (incantations), physical components (herbs, candles, etc.), and symbolic actions (tying knots, drawing symbols) to manifest the practitioner's intent.

The Ethics and Risks of Spellwork

In the practice of defensive magic, ethics can't be overstated. Just as in any form of defense, there's a thin line between protection and harm. Binding spells, for example, could be considered invasive or manipulative if applied without due consideration for the principles of free will and ethical conduct. Similarly, the misuse of banishing spells can inadvertently affect innocent parties. Therefore, spellwork must be approached responsibly and conscientiously.

While there are risks, such as the possible backfire of a spell or attracting unwanted attention from spiritual entities, careful preparation can mitigate these. The practitioner should take into account not only the ethical dimensions but also the potential consequences, both intended and unintended. This means being precise in your intention, methodical in your preparation, and respectful of all the energies and entities you may interact with.

Defensive magic and spellwork offer a vast array of techniques for psychic protection. Grounded in longstanding principles that have evolved across different cultural contexts, these methods enable individuals to employ a more proactive stance in safeguarding their psychic well-being. However, these practices come with their own set of ethical considerations and potential risks. The key to effective and responsible spellwork lies in understanding these complexities and navigating them with caution, respect, and wisdom.

CHAPTER 14: PLANT AND HERBAL ALLIES

While crystals, talismans, and intricate spells may constitute the more glamorous aspects of psychic defense, the botanical world offers a host of allies with equally potent protective abilities. Plants and herbs have been used for millennia in various traditions for both physical and metaphysical well-being. This chapter dives into how the power of plants can be harnessed to defend against psychic attacks and to fortify your energy field.

The Roots of Herbal Psychic Defense

Before discussing specific plants and their applications, it's essential to understand how deeply rooted the practice of using herbs for psychic protection is in human history. Various cultural traditions, including but not limited to Native American, African, and Asian practices, have revered the power of plants and incorporated them into their spiritual and defensive rituals. Even in Western medical traditions, the apothecary's arsenal often included herbs believed to have protective qualities against evil spirits and energies. Herbs like sage, rosemary, and mugwort were not just culinary or medicinal herbs but also considered potent in warding off negative energies.

Interestingly, science is starting to catch up, acknowledging the psychophysiological effects of certain plants. For example, research in phytochemistry has isolated specific plant compounds that influence the human nervous system, affecting mental states and emotions. Though not directly a "psychic" effect, this research does indicate that plants have a more substantial impact on us than previously thought, including possibly on our energetic bodies.

Botanicals for Protection, Grounding, and Shielding

To integrate plants into your psychic defense strategy, you can use them in various forms such as essential oils, dried herbs, or even as live plants in your living space. Below are some commonly used plants and their traditional applications in psychic defense:

- **Sage:** Perhaps the most famous for smudging rituals, burning sage is believed to cleanse spaces and auras of negative energies.
- **Lavender:** Known for its calming effects, lavender is

said to bring peace and tranquility, making it difficult for negative energies to penetrate your defenses.

- **Rosemary:** Used in various traditions to provide protective shields, rosemary is often used in sachets or incense. It is also said to enhance mental clarity, which could make you less susceptible to psychic manipulation.

- **Mugwort:** Traditionally used to enhance psychic abilities, it is also considered protective, especially during dream states or astral travel.

- **Black Tourmaline:** Though technically a mineral, it's worth mentioning in this context due to its frequent use in plant-based rituals for grounding and shielding against negativity.

It's crucial to remember that the effectiveness of these plants often depends on the practitioner's belief and intention. In other words, the plant itself is a tool, but your intent activates its potential. Always research and perhaps consult with an expert to ensure you are using plants in a manner that is safe, especially if you plan to ingest them or use them on your skin.

Incorporating Plants into Rituals and Everyday Life

You don't need to conduct elaborate rituals to benefit from the protective qualities of plants. Simple daily practices can be just as effective. For instance, you could diffuse essential oils in your living spaces or wear them on pulse points. Keeping live protective plants in your home or workspace can act as a living shield against negative energies. Some people also create sachets filled with a mix of protective herbs to carry with them or to place under their pillows.

For those who prefer rituals, a simple ceremony using a protective herb can be a potent act. For example, a ritual bath infused with rosemary and lavender can offer both psychic protection and spiritual cleansing. Mugwort can be stitched into dream pillows or dream catchers to protect during sleep and to encourage insightful dreams.

Plant and herbal allies offer an accessible and natural form of psychic defense that can easily be incorporated into daily life or specific rituals. Their role in various cultural traditions and emerging scientific research underscores their potential effectiveness. By using plants mindfully, you can build an additional layer of protection around your energy field and enrich your overall strategy for psychic defense. Whether you choose to burn sage, create herbal sachets, or infuse your bath with protective herbs, remember that your intention is the key to unlocking the plant's potential.

CHAPTER 15: SACRED GEOMETRY AND PSYCHIC DEFENSE

Sacred geometry, the study and application of geometric shapes and patterns with spiritual significance, has intrigued mathematicians, artists, and spiritual practitioners for centuries. Although rooted in mathematical principles, sacred geometry also taps into the realm of metaphysics, representing deeper cosmic truths and holding potential for spiritual defense mechanisms. This chapter will delve into how sacred geometry can be integrated into a comprehensive strategy for psychic defense.

The Mathematics Behind Sacred Geometry

At first glance, the incorporation of mathematics into psychic defense might seem incongruent. Yet, the discipline of sacred geometry demonstrates that certain shapes and patterns are recurrent in nature and have been revered across various civilizations for their mystical properties. The most commonly cited forms in sacred geometry include the circle, the square, and the triangle, as well as complex structures like the Flower of Life, the Platonic Solids, and the Fibonacci Sequence.

Mathematics offers the precision and universality that language often lacks. For example, the ratio of the Fibonacci Sequence (approximately 1.618033988749895, known as the Golden Ratio) is found in many natural phenomena, including the arrangement of leaves on a stem and the spiral pattern of galaxies. The Phi ratio, Pi, and other mathematical constructs reveal a level of symmetry and coherence in the universe that many believe is not mere chance but a form of cosmic intelligence or divine blueprint.

Metaphysical Applications for Psychic Defense

Sacred geometry is thought to possess particular energetic frequencies that can interact with human energy fields. By understanding and utilizing these geometric forms, it is possible to channel energies conducive to protection and defense. Below are some ways in which sacred geometry can be employed:

1. **Symbolic Visualization**: During meditation or contemplative exercises, one can visualize sacred geometric shapes to fortify their psychic defenses. For instance, envisioning oneself inside a protective

pyramid or sphere can provide a sense of shielding from external negative energies.

2. **Physical Representations**: Symbols of sacred geometry can be placed around living spaces, either as artworks, talismans, or etched forms. This is thought to create an energetic grid that repels negative influences.

3. **Ritual Incorporation**: Incorporating sacred geometry into rituals can amplify their efficacy. By using the correct geometric forms, the energy raised during ritualistic practices is believed to be better channeled and more focused, thereby strengthening the protective barriers one is attempting to establish.

It's essential to approach these applications with a level of sensitivity and respect for the forms themselves, understanding their historic and metaphysical significance. While the direct causal links between sacred geometry and psychic defense are not scientifically validated, countless anecdotal accounts suggest a level of effectiveness that merits consideration.

Cultural Contexts and Sacred Geometry

Sacred geometry is not limited to any single culture or religious practice. From the intricate Islamic geometric art forms to the mandalas in Hinduism and Buddhism, and the significance of the circle in Native American cultures, sacred geometry has a global resonance. Its ubiquity suggests that these geometric principles tap into universal truths that transcend cultural and geographical boundaries. By understanding the cultural contexts in which these shapes and patterns have been revered, one can gain deeper insights into their potential for psychic defense.

Sacred geometry offers an intricate and philosophically rich avenue for psychic defense. Its principles, grounded in mathematics but extending into the metaphysical, provide a toolkit of shapes and patterns believed to resonate with protective energies. Whether through visualization, physical representation, or ritualistic incorporation, these geometric forms can serve as another layer in a multifaceted approach to safeguarding one's energetic well-being. Understanding the cross-cultural significance of sacred geometry can further enrich its application in psychic defense, offering a universally resonant method for protection.

CHAPTER 16:
ARCHETYPAL AND
SYMBOLIC DEFENSE

Archetypes and symbols have been a part of human consciousness for thousands of years, deeply ingrained in our psyches. These powerful concepts manifest in various forms of cultural expression, including myths, legends, and even modern movies and books. This chapter explores how archetypes and symbols can serve as effective mechanisms in psychic defense, delving into the psychological implications and practical applications of these age-old constructs.

Archetypes as Psychological Defense Mechanisms

The idea of archetypes was notably elaborated by Swiss psychiatrist Carl Jung, who postulated that these universal symbols and themes reside in the collective unconscious—a layer of the unconscious mind shared among all humans. Archetypes like the Hero, the Mother, the Sage, and the Shadow are intrinsic to human storytelling and culture, and they also serve a psychological function by helping to structure our understanding of the world.

In the realm of psychic defense, invoking certain archetypes can be empowering. For example, adopting the mindset of the "Warrior" can instill a sense of courage and initiative, helping one to confront or repel psychic attacks. Similarly, summoning the archetype of the "Healer" could facilitate psychic self-care by encouraging nurturing behaviors. However, it's crucial to acknowledge the dual nature of archetypes; they possess both light and shadow aspects. While invoking the Warrior can foster resilience, it could also spur aggressive behaviors if not tempered with awareness and control.

Symbolic Constructs for Psychic Defense

Symbols, like archetypes, are powerful tools for the human mind. They can summarize complex concepts into easily recognizable forms, making them invaluable for rituals and visualization techniques, which are often used in psychic defense. The protective power of certain symbols—such as a circle, cross, or pentagram—has been respected across diverse cultures and spiritual traditions.

Using symbols in your psychic defense can be as straightforward as visualizing a protective bubble around you. Some people prefer to use more intricate symbols like a six-pointed star or even personalized sigils that they have created. When using symbols, the emotional and psychological connection to the symbol enhances its protective powers. For instance, if a certain religious or spiritual symbol is significant to you, incorporating it into your psychic defense strategy can strengthen your mental fortifications.

Integration of Archetypes and Symbols in Everyday Life

The real potency of archetypes and symbols comes from their integration into everyday life. Utilizing these tools for psychic defense shouldn't be an isolated practice but rather a part of a holistic approach to well-being. This can be achieved by:

1. Regular Meditation: Incorporating archetypal or symbolic visualizations into daily meditation routines can fortify your psychic defense mechanisms over time.

2. Mindful Interaction: Being conscious of the archetypal roles you and others play in interpersonal relationships can provide you valuable insights and offer ways to erect psychic defenses where necessary.

3. Creative Expression: Artistic endeavors like drawing, writing, or even acting can serve as outlets for engaging with these archetypes and symbols, thereby making their energies more accessible for psychic defense.

Archetypes and symbols offer powerful avenues for psychic defense due to their deep-rooted presence in the collective human psyche. Their psychological and emotional impact can be harnessed for protection through mindful practice and integration into one's daily life. By invoking the appropriate archetypes and employing meaningful symbols, you not only enhance your psychic defenses but also engage in a form of self-discovery, tapping into universal themes that have guided human behavior across millennia. These timeless tools not only act as shields against psychic intrusions but also serve as mirrors, reflecting the complexities of the human soul, thereby offering a route for both external protection and internal growth.

CHAPTER 17: PSYCHIC DEFENSE AND RELATIONSHIPS

In the realm of personal relationships, psychic defense takes on unique challenges and significance. Navigating complex human interactions while maintaining your energetic integrity requires a blend of mindfulness, skill, and practice. This chapter delves into the intricacies of sustaining psychic defense within relationships, specifically discussing how to protect oneself from the emotional and energetic drain often labeled as being caused by "energy vampires."

Identifying Energy Vampires

The term "energy vampire" has been used to describe people who seem to drain your emotional and psychic energy, leaving you feeling depleted, stressed, or overwhelmed. While it's important not to demonize individuals or imply malicious intent, the reality is that some people can, knowingly or unknowingly, tap into your energy field in a way that is exhausting. There are several signs that you are dealing with an energy vampire:

- **Constant Negativity**: They often express a consistently pessimistic view of life.
- **High Drama**: They seem to attract crisis or generate situations that require emotional investment from you.
- **Emotional Manipulation**: They guilt-trip or emotionally blackmail you into serving their needs, often at the cost of your well-being.

Building Psychic Boundaries in Relationships

1. **Mindful Communication**: The first step in maintaining psychic defense in a relationship is to establish clear boundaries. Openly and calmly express your needs and limits. Assertiveness, in this case, is not aggression but a way of maintaining your psychic hygiene.

2. **Energetic Shielding**: Utilize the energetic shielding techniques discussed in previous chapters, such as visualizing an aura of protective light around you, especially when you are about to engage with someone who drains your energy.

3. **Time Management**: Limit the amount of time spent with individuals who you find draining. It's crucial

to balance your commitments in a way that doesn't deplete your psychic reserves.

Strategies for Coping with Energy Vampires

- **Disengagement**: Sometimes the best defense is a tactical withdrawal. Stepping back physically or emotionally can protect your psychic space.
- **Grounding Techniques**: Grounding methods, like connecting with the earth element or engaging in physical activities, can help you replenish lost energy.
- **Consult Your Inner Circle**: Trusted friends or family can provide additional perspectives on the relationship, helping you understand if you're being unduly influenced or drained.

In certain situations, you may find it necessary to sever or distance yourself from relationships that are persistently harmful to your psychic health. Such decisions are difficult but crucial for your overall well-being.

The complex landscape of human relationships poses specific challenges to psychic defense. Knowing how to identify "energy vampires" and using techniques for building psychic boundaries can mitigate the risks. Whether through mindful communication, energetic shielding, or other coping strategies, safeguarding your energy within the relational sphere is a skill worth mastering. This serves not only to protect you but also to foster healthier, more balanced relationships with those around you.

CHAPTER 18:
DEFENSE AGAINST
COLLECTIVE PSYCHIC
PHENOMENA

The concept of psychic defense usually brings to mind images of personal shields and spiritual rituals designed to protect an individual from targeted psychic attacks or negative energies. However, there is an often-overlooked aspect that deserves attention: collective psychic phenomena. These are psychic and energetic events that affect a group of people, a community, or even a larger population. They can manifest as mass hysteria, shared delusions, or collective karma. In this chapter, we delve into the strategies to defend against these collective psychic phenomena, recognizing that individual well-being is interconnected with the larger societal and even global energetic landscape.

Understanding Collective Psychic Phenomena

Collective psychic phenomena differ from individual experiences in that they can affect a large group of people simultaneously. This doesn't mean that every individual in that group will be affected to the same degree, or even in the same manner, but the overarching energy or influence is shared.

1. **Mass Hysteria**: This is a phenomenon where a collective fear or belief spreads rapidly through a population, causing irrational behaviors and even physical symptoms. Historically, episodes like the Salem witch trials or the dancing plagues in Europe are cited as instances of mass hysteria.

2. **Shared Delusions**: This involves a group of people collectively holding onto a belief or perception that is disconnected from reality. This is often seen in cult-like settings but can also occur in less organized forms, such as urban legends or myths that a community holds.

3. **Collective Karma**: This is a concept prevalent in Eastern philosophies where the actions of a collective, such as a family, community, or nation, produce collective effects that are experienced by the group as a whole.

Defensive Strategies against Collective Phenomena

Because the energies involved in collective phenomena are vast and diffuse, traditional individual defense mechanisms like shielding or grounding may not be wholly effective. Here are some strategies:

1. **Heightened Awareness**: The first line of defense is always awareness. Being cognizant of collective energies allows you to act before you are unconsciously swept away. This could involve stepping back from media hysteria, evaluating facts critically, and avoiding emotional escalation.

2. **Collective Grounding Rituals**: These involve community-oriented rituals designed to ground collective energy. This could range from group meditations to participating in calming communal activities like tree-planting, to subtly shift the collective psychic energy.

3. **Invoking Higher Collective Consciousness**: Here, spiritual practices that call upon collective deities or energies for protection and guidance are useful. These can be in the form of prayers, chants, or even collective visualization practices aimed at lifting the collective energy.

Energetic Responsibility and Contribution

A crucial part of defending against collective psychic phenomena is understanding one's own contribution to that energy. Collective phenomena are, after all, the sum of individual contributions. Ethical and energetic responsibility starts at the personal level.

1. **Self-Check**: Regularly examine your emotional and

energetic states to ensure you are not unconsciously contributing to negative collective energies. This can be done through meditation or journaling.

2. **Positive Contributions**: Engage in actions that contribute positively to the collective energy. This can be as simple as acts of kindness or as complex as organizing community events aimed at healing and unity.

Collective psychic phenomena pose a unique set of challenges when it comes to psychic defense. They require not just individual actions but also collective efforts for effective mitigation. By understanding the nature of these phenomena, adopting multi-layered defensive strategies, and recognizing our own contributions to collective energies, we can better protect ourselves and contribute to the psychic well-being of our communities at large.

CHAPTER 19:
PSYCHIC DEFENSE
IN DIGITAL SPACES

The emergence of digital spaces has revolutionized the way we interact with each other and the world around us. However, the metaphysical implications of these spaces are often overlooked. The psychic energies that permeate physical environments also extend into digital realms. Consequently, psychic defense mechanisms that we deploy in the physical world may need to be adapted or extended to cover our digital interactions. This chapter delves into the unique considerations for psychic defense within digital spaces, such as social media, online forums, and even emails.

Digital Footprint and Energetic Residue

Just as physical objects and places can retain residual energy, digital spaces also have an energetic imprint. Every tweet, post, or comment we make online leaves an energetic trail that can be receptive to different kinds of psychic energies. Some people might be sensitive enough to perceive these subtle energies, whether positive or negative. As we engage in digital spaces, being conscious of the energies we are sending out and receiving can be crucial.

To manage your digital footprint's energetic residue, you might consider the following:

- Periodically review your digital history, deleting or archiving posts, comments, or interactions that no longer serve your best interests or that you perceive as energetically draining.
- Utilize privacy settings to limit the public's access to your personal information. In a metaphysical context, this acts as a form of digital shielding, preventing unauthorized energetic transactions.

Psychic Ties and Digital Interactions

Social media platforms enable us to connect with people around the globe instantaneously. However, they also make it easier to form psychic ties, intentionally or unintentionally. Psychic cords can be formed not just through physical interaction but also through digital communication. These cords, which are energetic links between individuals, can serve as channels for transferring various types of psychic energy.

Here are some steps you can take to manage psychic ties in digital spaces:

- Be selective with whom you interact. You're not obliged to accept every friend request or to follow back everyone who follows you.

- Regularly cleanse your digital spaces using visualization techniques or other psychic cleansing methods to sever unnecessary or harmful psychic cords. Imagine a light scanning your digital profile and severing unwanted cords as it moves along.

- Unfollow or mute accounts that consistently make you feel energetically drained or emotionally disturbed. Digital spaces should be curated to support your well-being.

Defensive Strategies Specific to Digital Platforms

Different digital platforms have their own unique set of energetic dynamics, and therefore, may require specialized defense strategies. For example, platforms like Twitter, known for fast-paced interactions and a broad reach, might expose you to a wider range of energies in a shorter amount of time. On the other hand, more personal platforms like direct messaging apps could make you more susceptible to focused, directed psychic attacks.

- For broader platforms: Use general shielding techniques that cover a wider range but may not be as intense. Imagine a filter surrounding your digital persona, letting in only positive interactions while deflecting negative ones.

- For more intimate platforms: Use more targeted shielding methods that are stronger but focused on specific kinds of interactions. These could include setting strong energetic boundaries or creating psychic "firewalls" to filter out unwanted energies.

By understanding the energetic dynamics of various platforms, you can tailor your defense strategies more effectively.

Digital spaces offer an array of opportunities and challenges in the context of psychic defense. The energetic residue left by digital footprints, the formation of psychic ties through online interactions, and the varying dynamics of different digital platforms all require thoughtful consideration and action. As our lives continue to integrate with the digital world, adapting our psychic defense strategies for these spaces becomes increasingly essential. The more conscious we become of our digital interactions and their psychic implications, the better we can protect our energetic well-being.

CHAPTER 20: THE ROLE OF PRAYER AND DIVINE ASSISTANCE IN PSYCHIC DEFENSE

While psychic defense often involves individual techniques such as shielding, grounding, and invoking spiritual allies, it's important to recognize the role of prayer and divine assistance as powerful tools for protecting one's energetic boundaries. This chapter delves into how these ancient practices can be integrated into a modern psychic defense strategy, discussing the conceptual underpinnings as well as practical applications.

The Conceptual Framework: Connecting to Higher Powers

Prayer and divine assistance operate under the premise that there are higher powers—be it God, gods, angels, ascended masters, or the universe at large—that can be invoked for guidance and protection. Whether you approach it from a monotheistic, polytheistic, or even a more abstract, spiritual standpoint, the central idea is the same: by seeking external divine help, one can fortify their psychic defenses.

The basis for invoking higher powers in psychic defense lies in the concept of interconnectedness. Many spiritual and religious traditions propose that all existence is interlinked, suggesting that individual energy fields are part of a greater cosmic network. In this framework, prayer serves as a form of energetic dialogue with the larger universe, aiming to align oneself with protective energies or entities.

Prayer Techniques in Psychic Defense

1. **Directed Prayer:** This involves clearly articulating what you're seeking protection from, and whom you're invoking for aid. It's essential to be as specific as possible—whether it's protection from a specific individual, a type of psychic attack, or a broader energetic issue.

2. **Affirmative Prayer:** Rather than requesting help or protection, affirmative prayer involves stating your desired outcome as if it has already occurred. This is based on the idea that affirming something as true helps to bring that reality into being.

3. **Meditative Prayer:** This form of prayer involves no spoken words. Instead, you focus your energy and thoughts on a higher power or the protective energy you wish to attract. Through this focused intent, you build a shield or layer of defense around yourself.

Regardless of the technique used, the most crucial factor is sincerity and a sense of purpose. Ritualistic prayers without genuine feeling are considered less effective in the energetic realm.

Application in Modern Life

In our modern world, prayer can often be overlooked or dismissed as an archaic practice with no scientific basis. However, numerous studies in the realm of psychology and even medicine have started to investigate the potential benefits of prayer and spirituality in coping with stress, illness, and other adversities. These emerging perspectives provide a secular support to the age-old spiritual practice, positioning it as a beneficial complement to more "earthly" methods of psychic defense.

Additionally, given that our world is more interconnected than ever, the energies we encounter are increasingly complex, originating from diverse cultures, technologies, and even virtual spaces. Divine assistance can serve as a universal protection, transcending man-made and cultural barriers to offer a form of psychic defense that is both comprehensive and individually tailored. Prayer can be performed anywhere, anytime, and requires no special tools—making it one of the most accessible forms of psychic defense.

Prayer and divine assistance serve as invaluable tools in an effective psychic defense strategy. By aligning oneself with higher powers or universal energies, individuals can tap into a cosmic reservoir of protective strength. Whether one opts for directed, affirmative, or meditative prayer, the key to effectiveness lies in genuine intent. In the context of a modern, interconnected world where traditional and digital energies constantly interact, these ancient practices offer a timeless, universally applicable layer of psychic defense.

CHAPTER 21: ASTRAL DEFENSE STRATEGIES

The astral plane, a dimension that exists parallel to the physical world, has been the subject of interest and exploration for millennia. From shamanic journeys to modern out-of-body experiences (OBEs), humans have ventured into this realm for various reasons, including spiritual enlightenment, knowledge gathering, and therapeutic healing. However, as with any other domain—physical or otherwise—risks are present. This chapter aims to focus on how you can protect yourself during such astral journeys or out-of-body experiences. We'll discuss what astral entities are, how to identify potential threats, and techniques to safeguard your energetic body in the astral realm.

Understanding Astral Entities

Entities in the astral plane can range from benevolent guides and ancestors to malicious beings who may attempt to interfere with or harm a traveler. While the nature and taxonomy of these entities can be a subject of both cultural interpretation and personal belief, it's generally accepted among those who practice astral travel that not every entity is benevolent.

Malicious entities may try to latch onto your astral body or create energetic cords, which can result in various negative consequences upon returning to the physical body. Such repercussions can include energetic drainage, emotional distress, or even physical ailments. It is important to recognize that, much like predatory animals in the wild, these entities are part of the astral ecology and are not "evil" in a moral sense. However, protecting oneself from them is a practical necessity.

Astral Defense Techniques

1. **Shielding**: Similar to the psychic shielding techniques discussed in previous chapters, before entering the astral realm, envision a protective bubble or sphere of light surrounding your astral body. This shield should be impenetrable and act as a barrier against unwanted entities or energies.

2. **Cord Cutting**: During or after your astral journey, you may notice energetic cords linking you to other entities or places in the astral plane. Visualize a tool like a sword or a pair of scissors to sever these cords decisively. Some practitioners recommend invoking a higher power or guide to assist in this.

3. **Sacred Geometry**: Using symbols like the Flower of Life, the Merkaba, or the Sri Yantra can add an additional layer of protection to your astral body. Visualize these symbols surrounding you or incorporate them into your shielding.

4. **Intention Setting**: Before embarking on an astral journey, clearly define your purpose and set strong intentions for protection. This provides a focus that can guide your actions in the astral plane and help repel undesired interference.

5. **Guided Assistance**: Call upon spiritual guides, ancestors, or higher powers you align with to accompany and protect you during the journey. This is similar to invoking divine assistance in prayer but tailored to astral travel.

Returning and Grounding

While it might be fascinating to explore the astral realm, returning safely to your physical body is crucial. Once back, grounding techniques such as consuming earthly foods, walking barefoot on natural ground, or engaging in focused breathing can help you integrate your experiences and shake off any residual astral energies.

Additionally, some practitioners recommend a cleansing ritual or energy clearing exercise after astral travel, to ensure that no undesirable elements have returned with you. Salt baths, smudging with sage, or working with grounding crystals like hematite can be useful for this purpose.

Astral travel offers a unique dimension of experience, but it comes with its own set of challenges and potential hazards.

By understanding the types of entities that inhabit the astral plane and equipping yourself with the appropriate defense techniques, you can safeguard your energetic well-being during these ethereal adventures. Whether it's through shielding, intention setting, or invoking higher guidance, adequate preparation is crucial for a safe and enriching astral journey.

CHAPTER 22:
PSYCHIC DEFENSE
FOR CHILDREN

As psychic defense gains attention in the world of adults, it's crucial not to overlook its significance for children. Young minds are often more open and sensitive to psychic phenomena, making them particularly vulnerable to psychic attacks or energy drains. This chapter provides guidance for parents and caregivers on how to educate children about protecting their energy fields.

Sensitizing Children to Psychic Concepts

The first step in teaching children psychic defense is helping them understand the very concept of energy and psychic phenomena. Unlike adults who might rely on complex theories or esoteric jargon, children resonate better with simplified explanations and analogies.

1. **The Energy Bubble**: You can start by telling children that each person has an "energy bubble" around them. This bubble can be happy or sad, strong or weak, and it's influenced by how we feel and who we interact with.

2. **Good and Bad Energies**: Explain that some people or situations make our energy bubble feel happy and strong, while others might make it feel sad or weak. The idea is to instill an early sense of energy discernment in them.

3. **Intuitive Signals**: Teach them to listen to their gut feelings. If they feel uneasy, scared, or drained around someone, they should understand that it might be because of conflicting energy interactions.

Basic Defense Mechanisms for Children

While it's not advisable to expose children to complex rituals, some simple, yet effective defense mechanisms can help them guard against psychic vulnerabilities.

1. **White Light Visualization**: Teach children to visualize a bright, white light surrounding them whenever they feel scared or uneasy. This light serves as a barrier against negative energies.

2. **Energy Grounding**: An uncomplicated grounding exercise could involve imagining roots extending from

their feet into the Earth, helping to anchor their energy.

3. **Positive Affirmations**: Simple affirmations like "I am strong," "I am safe," or "I am protected" can be incredibly empowering for children. Repeating these affirmations helps solidify their energy fields.

Creating Safe Spaces

In addition to teaching children basic defense mechanisms, it's also important to create a physically and energetically safe space for them.

1. **Physical Objects**: Items like dream catchers, protective stones, or even stuffed animals can be designated as "protective allies" for children. The belief in the object's protective qualities often boosts a child's psychic defense.

2. **Bedtime Rituals**: Incorporate a simple protection ritual into their bedtime routine, like saying a protective prayer or chanting a short affirmation.

3. **Energetic Cleaning**: Teach them about the importance of cleaning their space energetically. For instance, they can help you "sweep away bad energies" during regular house cleaning. The symbolic act of sweeping or dusting can serve as an easy-to-understand form of energy clearing for children.

Protecting children from psychic vulnerabilities requires a simplified yet sensitive approach. Educating them about the basics of energy fields, teaching straightforward defense mechanisms, and creating safe spaces can go a long way in instilling a sense of security and resilience. Just as we teach children to defend themselves in the physical world —like looking both ways before crossing a street or not talking to strangers—the need for psychic defense is becoming increasingly clear in a world where energies, both positive and negative, interact with us constantly.

CHAPTER 23:
PSYCHIC DEFENSE
FOR ANIMALS

Animals, much like humans, possess energy fields that are susceptible to various forms of psychic phenomena. While the degree to which animals are aware of or can interact with psychic energies is a topic of debate, there is a general consensus among practitioners and experts in the field that animals can be vulnerable to psychic influences and attacks. In this chapter, we will explore the nuances of animal susceptibility to psychic phenomena, strategies to fortify their psychic defenses, and methods for cleansing their energy fields.

Recognizing Vulnerability in Animals

One of the primary challenges in psychic defense for animals is recognizing when an animal is under psychic stress or attack. Unlike humans, animals can't verbalize their experiences, so it requires keen observation and a deep understanding of an animal's behavior to identify irregularities that may indicate psychic disturbances.

Behavioral Signs: Changes in behavior, such as increased aggression, withdrawal, or unusual restlessness, can signify that an animal is experiencing psychic discomfort. Some animals may also vocalize more than usual or engage in repetitive behaviors.

Physical Signs: While physical symptoms like lethargy or digestive issues could have medical causes, they can also suggest psychic disturbances if they appear suddenly and without apparent reason.

Environmental Clues: An animal's environment can also give clues about psychic attacks. For example, if an animal suddenly avoids a specific part of its living area where it used to spend time, there may be negative energy concentrated there.

Psychic Defense Techniques for Animals

Implementing psychic defense for animals incorporates some methods similar to those used for humans, adapted to accommodate the unique physiology and psychology of animals.

Shielding Techniques

Visualizing a protective energy shield around the animal can be useful. As you concentrate, picture the shield emanating from the animal and extending outwards. Some practitioners also incorporate physical touch, such as placing a hand on the animal while projecting a shield, to facilitate the energy transfer.

Crystals and Talismans

Just as crystals and talismans can be used for human psychic defense, certain stones and objects can also offer protection for animals. Black tourmaline, for instance, is often used near an animal's sleeping area to ward off negative energies.

Rituals and Energy Cleansing

Performing regular energy-cleansing rituals can benefit animals as much as humans. Smudging with sage or using sound therapy like chimes or Tibetan singing bowls can cleanse an animal's aura.

Importance of Routine and Consistency

Animals thrive on routine and predictability, and this extends to psychic defense strategies. Consistency in implementing techniques, whether it's regularly refreshing a protective shield or periodic energy cleansing, contributes to an effective defense. The psychic field of an animal is often less complex but also less guarded than that of a human. Therefore, constant reinforcement is essential for maintaining a stable energy field.

Protecting animals from psychic phenomena is an often-overlooked yet essential aspect of holistic well-being for your pets or animal companions. Recognizing the signs of psychic stress or attack in animals is the first step in implementing an effective defense strategy. Techniques such as shielding, use of crystals, and energy-cleansing rituals can be adapted to suit animals. Remember, consistency is key; maintaining a regular regimen of these practices is essential for fortifying your animal's psychic defenses effectively. By paying attention to the psychic well-being of your animal companions, you not only enhance their quality of life but also deepen the interspecies bonds of understanding and care.

CHAPTER 24:
WORKPLACE
PSYCHIC DEFENSE

Methods to Employ Psychic Defense Strategies in Professional Environments

In most aspects of modern life, maintaining psychic defenses has become increasingly critical. Workplaces are no exception; in fact, they can often be hotbeds of psychic interaction. While we frequently consider workplace issues in terms of tangible factors like workload, job security, and interpersonal relationships, psychic vulnerabilities can play an overlooked role in affecting one's mental and emotional state. This chapter delves into the necessity of psychic defense in the workplace and provides strategies to shield yourself energetically while navigating the complexities of professional environments.

Assessing the Psychic Environment of Your Workplace

The first step in implementing psychic defense in the workplace is a thorough assessment of your work environment. While some workplaces may be generally uplifting and positive, others might feel draining, aggressive, or stifling. Understanding the psychic tone of your workplace is key to identifying the kinds of psychic defenses you'll need. This involves observing the behavior and actions of your colleagues and superiors and noticing how these interactions impact your psychic energy. It's essential to discern whether the negative energies are arising from individuals who may be unwittingly directing their own stresses and fears towards you or whether there's a broader collective energy in the workplace that needs to be addressed.

Practical Psychic Defense Techniques for the Workplace

Psychic defense strategies can be effectively applied within the context of work, but they may require certain modifications to be unobtrusive and professionally appropriate. Here are some methods tailored for the workplace:

1. **Grounding Exercises**: Use quick grounding techniques that can be done sitting at your desk. This could be as simple as pressing your feet firmly into the ground while taking a few deep breaths.

2. **Shielding Practices**: Imaginatively create an energy shield around you before entering a meeting or dealing with a challenging task. This mental construct can act

as a psychic filter, allowing only positive energies to pass through.

3. **Selective Engagement**: Be cautious with whom you share personal information or deep emotional insights. This conserves your psychic energy and prevents others from tapping into your vulnerabilities.

4. **Energy Resets**: Take short breaks to step outside, connect with nature, or meditate briefly. These activities act as mini psychic cleanses, essential for maintaining a balanced energy field.

Harmonizing Workspace Energies

Your immediate workspace can also act as a conduit or a barrier for psychic energies. Pay attention to the physical arrangement and the energetic atmosphere of your workspace. Incorporating elements like plants, crystals, or symbolic objects can subtly enhance your psychic defense. This can be especially helpful if you have a stationary workspace. If your job involves moving around, consider carrying a small talisman or symbol with you that can act as a portable shield. Additionally, setting the intention for your workspace—mentally declaring it as a sanctuary for your psychic well-being—can provide an extra layer of defense.

Workplaces can either sustain or deplete your psychic energy, making psychic defense crucial in professional settings. Assessing the psychic environment, applying specific defense techniques, and harmonizing the energies of your workspace are strategic steps toward preserving your psychic integrity at work. By integrating these methods, you not only protect your own psychic field but also contribute to establishing a more positive, balanced, and productive work environment.

CHAPTER 25:
PSYCHIC DEFENSE
IN HEALTHCARE

Healthcare settings are unique environments where the confluence of emotional, physical, and sometimes, spiritual energies is especially potent. Physicians, nurses, and other healthcare professionals are frequently in close contact with individuals who are experiencing varying levels of emotional and physical distress. These practitioners are often considered the frontline defense in physical health but may overlook the importance of psychic defense in such intensive environments. This chapter aims to delve into the nuances of applying psychic defense principles in medical and caregiving settings, a critical area often neglected in mainstream discussions.

The Vulnerability of Healthcare Workers

Healthcare workers are often at a higher risk for psychic vulnerabilities due to the nature of their jobs. They are routinely exposed to the intense emotions and psychological states of their patients. This exposure can sometimes act like a sponge, absorbing the myriad forms of energies around them. A lack of psychic defense can lead to emotional exhaustion, decreased empathy, and even professional burnout.

Moreover, the healthcare setting is not just a meeting place for various human energies but also incorporates an array of technological equipment, from MRI machines to cardiac monitors. These devices emit electromagnetic fields that, while generally considered safe, could potentially influence the psychic energies in the environment. While the scientific community hasn't reached a consensus on the impact of these electromagnetic fields on psychic energies, being aware of their presence is important for a comprehensive psychic defense strategy.

Techniques Tailored for Healthcare Settings

1. **Shielding During Patient Interactions**: When healthcare workers engage with patients, it's crucial to establish a psychic shield to maintain emotional boundaries. This can be done through visualization techniques, such as imagining a protective bubble or shield around oneself. Unlike generic shielding, the intention here can be more focused—keeping out negative energies while allowing compassion and

healing energies to flow freely.

2. **Cleansing Rituals Between Shifts**: Given the high-stress nature of healthcare jobs, a cleansing ritual can be beneficial. This could be as simple as washing hands mindfully, visualizing negative energies going down the drain, or as elaborate as a short meditative session using protective crystals like black tourmaline or smoky quartz.

3. **Group Energy Harmonization**: Teamwork is often the backbone of healthcare settings. Synchronizing energies among team members can create a harmonious work environment. Simple group exercises, like synchronized breathing or collective visualization of positive outcomes for patients, can achieve this.

The Importance of Self-Care

Self-care is paramount for healthcare providers, not just for their own well-being but also to ensure they can provide the best care for their patients. Scheduled breaks for grounding exercises, energy renewal meditations, or even a brief walk outdoors can be instrumental in maintaining a balanced energy field. These are not frivolous activities but essential maintenance procedures for anyone committed to healthcare. The idea is not just to protect oneself but to create a resonance of well-being that positively influences both colleagues and patients.

Nutrition should not be overlooked, as the foods consumed can either fortify or deplete one's energy. Foods rich in life force energies, often called "prana" in some traditions, like fresh fruits and vegetables, can be included in the diet for better energy balance.

Healthcare environments are particularly charged with a mix of emotional, physical, and technological energies that make psychic defense crucial for the well-being of practitioners. Techniques like specialized psychic shielding, energy harmonization among team members, and personal self-care rituals are not just beneficial but essential for maintaining a balanced, harmonious environment. These practices do not just serve the individual healthcare worker but ripple out to affect the team and, most importantly, the patients in care. By adopting a mindful approach to psychic defense, healthcare providers can offer a deeper level of care that extends beyond physical healing to encompass emotional and psychic well-being.

CHAPTER 26: THE ROLE OF DIET AND NUTRITION IN PSYCHIC DEFENSE

The influence of diet and nutrition on physical health is widely understood and backed by extensive scientific research. However, the intersection of dietary choices with psychic or energetic well-being is less commonly considered but is no less important. This chapter delves into the role of diet and nutrition in bolstering psychic defenses, offering insights into foods that may serve to enhance or diminish your energetic field. While traditional dietary guidelines focus on macronutrients like proteins, fats, and carbohydrates, we will extend our scope to include micronutrients and the energetic quality of foods.

Macronutrients and Energy Resilience

The three primary macronutrients—proteins, fats, and carbohydrates—play different roles in physical health, and they may also contribute to psychic defense in various ways. Protein, for example, serves as a building block for cells and tissues, but it also acts as a foundational element for the energetic body. Diets rich in high-quality protein, derived from ethical and sustainable sources, can potentially contribute to a robust energetic field. Fats, especially omega-3 fatty acids found in fish, chia seeds, and flaxseeds, have been shown to improve brain function and mood regulation, which may, in turn, help fortify psychic barriers. Carbohydrates should be consumed in moderation, with a focus on complex carbohydrates like whole grains and vegetables, as they offer sustained energy that can be vital in maintaining a stable energetic field.

Micronutrients and Elemental Balancing

Micronutrients such as vitamins and minerals play a crucial role in physiological processes, many of which have a corresponding energetic function. For example, calcium is not just essential for bone health; in energetic terms, it is thought to aid in grounding the body. Magnesium, known for its calming effects on the nervous system, can also serve to stabilize an erratic energetic field. Foods rich in antioxidants, such as berries and green tea, are thought to act as psychic "scavengers," neutralizing free radicals not just in the physical body but also in the aura. It's worth considering that many micronutrients are better absorbed from whole foods rather than supplements, suggesting a focus on a well-balanced, nutrient-rich diet.

Energetic Quality of Foods

The concept of the energetic quality of foods is deeply rooted in various traditional systems of medicine, such as Ayurveda and Traditional Chinese Medicine (TCM). While the scientific framework for understanding these energies is still developing, anecdotal evidence and experiential knowledge offer some insights. Foods that are fresh, organic, and prepared with a sense of mindfulness are generally considered to have high energetic quality. These foods could act as enhancers of one's energetic field, making it more resilient to psychic intrusion. On the contrary, processed foods, genetically modified organisms (GMOs), and foods laden with artificial preservatives are seen as energetically "dead" or even detrimental to one's psychic defenses.

The role of diet and nutrition in psychic defense is multifaceted and extends beyond conventional understanding of macronutrients and micronutrients. Incorporating high-quality proteins, healthy fats, and complex carbohydrates can build a foundational resilience that supports both the physical and energetic body. Attention to micronutrients, obtained preferably from whole foods, can fine-tune the elemental balance within the energetic field. Lastly, acknowledging the energetic quality of foods and opting for those that are fresh, organic, and prepared with mindfulness can offer an additional layer of psychic protection. The adage "you are what you eat" seems to hold merit not just in the realm of physical health but also in the nuanced world of psychic defense.

CHAPTER 27: PSYCHIC DEFENSE DURING SLEEP AND DREAMS

Sleep and dream states are periods during which our conscious mind takes a backseat, allowing our subconscious to flourish. While this is essential for psychological well-being and cognitive processing, these states also make us susceptible to various types of psychic intrusions. This chapter aims to elucidate methods and practices that can be employed to ensure psychic safety during sleep and dreams.

The Vulnerability of the Sleep State

When we sleep, our physical bodies are at rest, but our psychic and energetic systems remain active. Traditional belief systems often describe this as a time when the "astral body" or "spirit" is more free to roam. Whether or not one adheres to these metaphysical explanations, the fact remains that our intuitive and psychic defenses are less guarded during sleep. This relaxed state may invite various forms of psychic interferences, ranging from unintentional energy transfers to deliberate psychic attacks.

In dream states, the vulnerability can be even more pronounced. This is because dreams are the language of our subconscious, rich in symbolism and emotional content. Psychic intrusions during this time can be confusing and disturbing, as they mingle with our own dream narratives. The complexity of dreams makes them a potent avenue for psychic phenomena to manifest, either positively or negatively. Therefore, understanding how to protect oneself during these vulnerable periods becomes imperative.

Techniques for Psychic Defense in Sleep

Several practices can be employed to fortify psychic defenses during sleep. Here are some strategies:

1. **Pre-Sleep Rituals**: Develop a calming pre-sleep routine that incorporates psychic self-defense methods. This could include a brief meditation, visualization of protective barriers, or even the use of protective talismans placed near the bed or under the pillow.

2. **Intention Setting**: Before sleeping, set clear intentions for psychic protection. Affirmations can be powerful tools in this context. You could say something like, "I am protected in my sleep, and only positive energies

can interact with me."

3. **Shielding Techniques**: Employ advanced psychic shielding techniques tailored for sleep. For example, envisioning a cocoon of white light around your sleeping form can serve as a formidable barrier against psychic intrusions.

4. **Environmental Safeguards**: Ensure that the sleeping environment is conducive to psychic safety. This could include using salt lines around the bed, protective herbs, or crystals like amethyst known for their calming and protective properties.

5. **Dream Recall and Analysis**: Keeping a dream journal can help you track any patterns or recurrent themes that may hint at psychic disturbances. Over time, this will help you identify what might be a psychic intrusion versus ordinary dream content.

The Importance of Dream Analysis

While defense techniques are vital, equally crucial is the role of dream analysis. A nuanced understanding of your own dream language can be an invaluable tool for distinguishing between psychic interference and subconscious processing. This understanding equips you to actively engage with your dreams, perhaps through practices like lucid dreaming, to assert control and set boundaries. It can also serve as an early warning system, making you aware of potential psychic vulnerabilities that you might need to address in your waking life.

Sleep and dream states are periods of heightened psychic vulnerability due to the relaxed state of our conscious defenses and the active engagement of our subconscious. A combination of pre-sleep rituals, intention setting, shielding techniques, and environmental safeguards can be employed for psychic protection. Incorporating dream analysis alongside these strategies can offer a robust defense mechanism, allowing for a more nuanced understanding of psychic phenomena that may occur during these states. With these tools in hand, you can approach sleep not only as a time for physical rest but also as a period secure from psychic intrusions.

CHAPTER 28:
DEFENSE AGAINST
PSYCHIC SCAMS
AND FRAUD

While exploring the realms of psychic phenomena, magic, and energy work, it's crucial to remember that not everyone you encounter will have your best interests at heart. The promise of unlocking psychic powers or providing an easy solution to life's problems has enticed many, and unfortunately, some individuals and organizations exploit this curiosity for financial or manipulative gains. This chapter aims to arm you with the necessary knowledge and critical thinking skills to identify, avoid, and defend against psychic scams and fraudulent practices.

Recognizing Red Flags

Psychic scams often carry specific indicators that can tip you off to their deceptive nature. Here are some common red flags:

- **Exorbitant Costs**: If the psychic or service demands a hefty sum right away, especially without offering any substantiation for their claims, be cautious. Authentic practitioners often provide some form of free initial consultation or lower-cost services to establish trust and prove their abilities.
- **Fear Tactics**: Be wary of anyone who instills a sense of impending doom or severe negativity that can only be removed through their exclusive services or products.
- **Vague or General Statements**: Fraudulent psychics often use "cold reading" techniques that involve making vague statements that could apply to anyone but seem personal.

Technological Avenues for Scams

The digital age has provided scammers with more platforms to reach potential victims. Email spam with headlines like "Unlock Your Psychic Potential" or "Secret to Love and Wealth Revealed" may lead to fraudulent schemes. Similarly, social media and websites full of overblown testimonials and impossible promises should be scrutinized. Always research thoroughly, read reviews, and ideally, get recommendations from trusted sources before engaging in any psychic services online.

Cybersecurity measures are also essential here. Make sure the website is secure (look for "https" in the URL), especially if financial transactions are involved. Maintain different passwords for different platforms to minimize the risk if one service turns out to be fraudulent.

Legal Recourse and Reporting

If you suspect that you've fallen victim to a psychic scam, you should take immediate action. Here are the steps involved:

- **Document Evidence**: Keep records of all communications, transactions, and any other evidence that might help your case.
- **Contact Authorities**: Depending on your jurisdiction, different agencies may be responsible for handling fraud cases, including psychic scams. This may include local police, federal agencies, or specialized units dealing with cybercrime or fraud.
- **Financial Institutions**: Inform your bank or credit card company about the fraudulent transactions as they may be able to assist in recovering funds and preventing further unauthorized activity.
- **Awareness**: Share your experiences (while maintaining anonymity if you wish) to warn others. Online forums, social media, and local community boards can be effective platforms for this.

Guarding against psychic scams is an integral part of your overall psychic defense strategy. While the quest for spiritual and psychic development is commendable, it should not overshadow the need for practical vigilance. Always be cautious when approached with grandiose claims, especially those requiring immediate financial commitments. Utilize digital tools wisely, being wary of unsolicited emails or flashy websites promising miraculous psychic abilities or solutions to life's complex problems. Finally, know the available legal channels to report scams and perhaps prevent others from becoming victims. By incorporating these protective measures, you arm yourself not just psychically but also practically against predatory elements in the psychic and magical realms.

CHAPTER 29:
PSYCHIC DEFENSE IN
CULTURAL CONTEXTS

Understanding psychic defense is not a one-size-fits-all endeavor. In fact, the approach to psychic defense can vary considerably depending on cultural context. This chapter delves into the intricacies of how different cultures perceive and practice psychic defense. We'll explore traditional techniques from various global traditions and examine the role that cultural beliefs and practices play in shaping psychic defense mechanisms.

Indigenous Beliefs and Psychic Defense

Indigenous cultures around the world have a rich heritage of spiritual practices and beliefs that often include methods for psychic defense. These might manifest in the form of rituals, shamanic practices, or the use of talismans and amulets imbued with protective energies. In many indigenous cultures, the shaman or spiritual healer holds the responsibility for the psychic well-being of the community. The shaman's role involves identifying and nullifying psychic threats, often through the use of chants, dances, and plant medicines. The community itself might participate in collective rituals to strengthen the psychic defenses of the entire group.

It is important to approach the psychic defense methods of indigenous cultures with the utmost respect and sensitivity. These practices are deeply rooted in their historical and spiritual context, and it would be inappropriate to appropriate these methods without a deep understanding and permission from the culture in question. It's also vital to consider that what may be effective in one cultural setting may not necessarily translate into another due to differences in underlying belief systems and worldviews.

Eastern Traditions and Psychic Defense

Eastern philosophies such as Buddhism, Hinduism, and Taoism have their own sets of practices for psychic defense. Concepts like karma, chi, and the chakras offer nuanced frameworks for understanding psychic interactions. For example, the idea of karma in both Buddhism and Hinduism can serve as a form of psychic defense; the belief that negative actions will result in negative outcomes might deter potential psychic attacks.

Practices like Tai Chi, Qi Gong, and various forms of meditation are commonly utilized to balance chi or prana, the life energy that flows through everyone. By maintaining a balanced and flowing life force, individuals can naturally bolster their psychic defenses. Chakra work, especially focusing on the solar plexus and heart chakras, can also offer layers of protection against psychic intrusions. Methods for shielding in Eastern traditions often focus on cultivating inner harmony so that negative energies find it difficult to penetrate the psychic defenses.

Western Esoteric Traditions and Psychic Defense

Western esoteric traditions, encompassing practices like Wicca, Kabbalah, and Hermeticism, offer another set of tools for psychic defense. These often involve ceremonial rituals, invocation of protective deities or archangels, and the use of sacred geometry and sigils for shielding. In the Kabbalistic tradition, for instance, specific sequences of Hebrew letters and invocations can be used for protection. Wiccan practices might include casting a circle and calling upon the elements for defense. Hermetic principles like "As above, so below" imply that creating physical talismans can have a real effect on the psychic realm.

It's worth noting that Western esoteric practices often draw from a melting pot of influences, including Christian, Jewish, Islamic, and even ancient Egyptian spiritual practices. This eclectic mix allows for a highly personalized approach to psychic defense, where practitioners can borrow elements from various traditions to create a defense strategy that resonates with them.

Cultural contexts provide a rich tapestry of psychic defense mechanisms and beliefs. Whether one is drawn to the shamanic practices of indigenous cultures, the energy balancing methods of Eastern philosophies, or the ritualistic approaches of Western esoteric traditions, understanding the cultural nuances is crucial. While borrowing techniques across cultures can enrich one's personal psychic defense strategies, it should be done so respectfully, ethically, and with a thorough understanding of the cultural implications. As with all aspects of psychic defense, the key is to find a personalized approach that aligns with one's own beliefs, experiences, and challenges.

CHAPTER 30: PSYCHIC DEFENSE AND PARANORMAL PHENOMENA

Our understanding of psychic defense has covered a broad swath of topics, from the esoteric nuances of energy fields to practical methodologies like shielding and grounding. While most discussions have revolved around human-generated psychic phenomena or self-induced states, this chapter takes a detour into a domain that has intrigued mankind for generations: paranormal phenomena. Encounters with so-called "ghosts," "spirits," or "entities" from other dimensions can have psychic implications, some of which may necessitate unique defense strategies.

Encounters with the Paranormal: An Overview

The term "paranormal" encompasses a wide array of phenomena that lie beyond the scope of scientific explanation, at least as of our current understanding. Whether one discusses ghosts haunting an old mansion, poltergeist activity, or even cryptids like the Mothman, the paranormal has always been a subject shrouded in mystery and skepticism. Yet, people from various cultures and walks of life report inexplicable experiences that go beyond mere hallucination or hoax. If we operate under the assumption that at least some of these experiences are genuine, it behooves us to consider the psychic impact these entities can have.

In many cases, individuals report a shift in energy or mood during paranormal encounters. Some feel drained or sense a heavy atmosphere; others describe being overcome with emotions that aren't their own. These experiences can bear similarities to psychic attacks or psychic energy "vampirism." Paranormal entities, given their unique nature, could influence our psychic state without necessarily subscribing to the human ethical or spiritual constructs we understand. This makes it essential to consider specialized defense mechanisms tailored to these extraordinary situations.

Psychic Defense Strategies for Paranormal Encounters

1. **Preemptive Energy Cleansing:** One of the most straightforward approaches is to regularly cleanse spaces known for paranormal activity. Rituals often

used for psychic defense, like sage smudging or the use of salt, can also deter negative paranormal entities.

2. **Enhanced Shielding:** Your usual psychic shields may need reinforcement when dealing with entities of a paranormal nature. Visualizing an impenetrable shield made from materials believed to repel negative energies, such as iron or obsidian, can offer heightened protection.

3. **Calling Upon Higher Powers:** This may include any divine figures, ancestors, or higher vibrational entities that align with your belief system. The crucial point is that the entities you invoke should resonate with positive energies capable of countering paranormal entities.

4. **Divination and Surveillance:** Tools like pendulums, dowsing rods, or even specialized technology can be employed to gauge the level and nature of paranormal activity in an area. Knowing your "enemy" is part of the battle, and this informational groundwork can help tailor your psychic defenses effectively.

5. **Collective Energy Pooling:** When facing phenomena that seem overwhelming, combining energy resources with other individuals can create a more potent defense. This collective shield not only amplifies the protection but also offers emotional support, which can be crucial in such high-stake situations.

The Importance of Adaptability

Paranormal entities, by their very nature, defy easy categorization or understanding. Unlike human sources of psychic disruption, we cannot readily predict their behaviors or motivations. This inherent unpredictability makes adaptability key in your defense strategy. You may need to combine techniques, modify existing ones, or even invent new approaches on the fly. It is advisable to keep an open mind and remain flexible, both in your practices and your beliefs, as new experiences may challenge existing paradigms.

Paranormal phenomena present a distinct set of challenges in the realm of psychic defense. Given the unpredictable and often powerful nature of these entities, standard defense mechanisms may not suffice. Enhancing existing techniques, employing specialized tools, and even relying on collective energies may be necessary. Most importantly, an adaptable mindset can serve you well in these extraordinary circumstances. Even as we tread carefully in realms that science has yet to fully explain, the application of specialized psychic defenses can provide some semblance of security and empowerment.

CHAPTER 31: LONG-TERM STRATEGIES FOR PSYCHIC DEFENSE

The majority of the book has explored various facets of psychic defense, from understanding energy fields to employing specific techniques for immediate protection. However, as you may have already gleaned, psychic defense is not a one-time effort but an ongoing process that requires sustained commitment and evolving strategies. This chapter focuses on long-term strategies that aim to continuously reinforce your psychic defenses and help maintain your energetic health over time.

Developing a Routine

One of the most straightforward ways to sustain your psychic defenses is to integrate psychic protection into your daily routine. A daily ritual of grounding, shielding, and purifying your energy field can go a long way. The routine could be as simple as spending a few minutes each morning visualizing a protective aura around yourself or invoking higher powers to guide and protect you throughout the day. The key is consistency; the more you practice, the stronger and more automatic your psychic defenses become.

In addition to daily practices, weekly or monthly rituals can help to intensify and deepen your psychic protection. These could involve more elaborate ceremonies, using talismans and crystals, or performing spellwork designed for long-term protection. Make sure these rituals are noted in your calendar to ensure they are not skipped or forgotten. Over time, you'll notice these practices becoming as essential to your well-being as any other form of self-care.

Continuous Learning and Adaptation

The landscape of psychic phenomena is dynamic and ever-changing, influenced by personal development, collective consciousness, and even technological advances. Consequently, your strategies for psychic defense must also adapt over time.

Continuous learning is crucial. Keep yourself updated with new techniques, tools, and theories in the field of psychic defense. This could be through reading books, attending workshops, or engaging in discussions with others interested in psychic phenomena. Even within this field, schools of thought and methodologies are continually evolving, and newer, perhaps more effective, techniques are being developed. Adapting your strategies accordingly ensures that you stay ahead of potential threats and vulnerabilities.

Don't be afraid to modify or even discard old techniques if they no longer serve you well. Be aware that as you evolve, your energy field changes, and so does its interaction with external forces. Therefore, a technique that was highly effective a few years ago might lose its efficacy. It is essential to assess the relevance and effectiveness of your psychic defense tools and strategies regularly.

Mental and Emotional Resilience

Long-term psychic defense is closely related to your overall mental and emotional well-being. Just as your physical health can impact your susceptibility to illness, your mental state can influence your vulnerability to psychic attacks or disturbances.

Cultivate mental resilience through mindfulness practices, meditation, and emotional intelligence training. The more balanced and centered you are, the less likely you are to be affected by external energies. Emotional resilience, developed through self-reflection and emotional processing, can act as a buffer against emotional or psychic vampires. Remember, a strong mind is a well-defended one.

Long-term strategies for psychic defense involve more than just the occasional ritual or the use of a talisman; they require a comprehensive, evolving approach that incorporates daily practices, continuous learning, and overall mental and emotional resilience. By integrating psychic defense into your routine, staying updated with new developments in the field, and fostering mental and emotional strength, you build a robust and durable shield against psychic disturbances. This integrated, long-term strategy equips you with the tools to navigate a complex, ever-changing psychic landscape, thereby ensuring your energetic well-being for years to come.

CHAPTER 32: PSYCHIC DEFENSE FOR PLACES AND LOCATIONS

While much of this book has focused on personal psychic defense, the concept extends beyond the individual to encompass places and locations. Various settings, like homes, workplaces, or sacred sites, also possess unique energetic imprints that can be influenced by psychic phenomena. This chapter delves into methods for cleansing and protecting these specific environments.

Psychic Resonance in Places

Every location has an energy field, influenced by its history, its occupants, and the activities that have taken place there. When a location has been subject to negative energies—whether from emotional conflicts, psychic attacks, or other sources—these energies can linger, affecting everyone who enters the space. This is sometimes termed as "psychic residue." Some haunted places, for instance, are thought to have an accumulation of psychic energies, often the result of tragic or violent events.

Identifying the Need for Cleansing

If you sense unease, excessive fatigue, or negative emotions in a particular place, or if electronic devices behave erratically, these could be indicators of a need for psychic cleansing. Additionally, some individuals with psychic sensitivities might perceive unsettling images or feelings in these locations. Pay attention to pets as well; animals can be sensitive to energies and might act strangely in spaces that require cleansing.

Cleansing Techniques

Smudging

Smudging involves burning herbs like sage, cedar, or sweetgrass, and using the smoke to purify the area. The ritual comes from indigenous cultures and has been adopted widely in modern spiritual practices. However, it's important to approach this practice with respect for its cultural origins. To smudge a space, light the bundled herb and pass it around the room, paying particular attention to corners, doorways, and windows where negative energy might accumulate.

Salt and Water

Salt is often considered a purifying agent. Some traditions recommend sprinkling sea salt or Himalayan salt at entrances or corners. Similarly, blessed or moon-charged water can be used to cleanse a space. It's commonly spritzed around the room or used to wipe down surfaces.

Sound Healing

Sound can shift energies in a room. Bells, gongs, and tuning forks are commonly used, but even your voice intoning specific chants or affirmations can serve to cleanse the space. The key is to focus on frequencies that are traditionally associated with purification or balance.

Crystals and Talismans

Quartz crystals, black tourmaline, and other stones can also be used to cleanse and protect spaces. These can be placed strategically around a room, or in some cases, buried at the four corners of a property. Talismans with protective symbols can also be hung or placed in strategic locations.

Ongoing Maintenance

Once a space is cleansed, it requires regular upkeep to maintain its energetic purity. Depending on the level of psychic activity, you might need to cleanse the area monthly, quarterly, or even weekly. Keeping live plants, utilizing natural light, and ensuring proper airflow can contribute to a sustained positive environment.

Protecting and cleansing the energy of specific places and locations is an essential extension of personal psychic defense strategies. From identifying the need for cleansing to employing various techniques like smudging, salt, and sound healing, you can significantly improve the energetic quality of your environment. Regular upkeep is necessary to maintain this purified state, ensuring that the space remains a sanctuary for all who enter. By being proactive in your approach to psychic defense in places and locations, you not only safeguard yourself but also create harmonious spaces that benefit everyone.

CHAPTER 33: THE INTERSECTION OF PSYCHOLOGY AND PSYCHIC DEFENSE

The interplay between psychology and psychic defense is a labyrinthine tapestry woven with threads of consciousness, perception, emotion, and the esoteric. While psychology is often rooted in empiricism, psychic phenomena often hinge on the unobservable, the extrasensory, or the not-yet-explained. However, the two domains are not entirely separate; rather, they inform and interact with each other in compelling ways. This chapter aims to explore this intricate relationship, examining how psychological constructs can be useful in understanding and applying psychic defense techniques, and vice versa.

The Psychological Basis of Psychic Phenomena

It is noteworthy that many aspects of psychic phenomena are closely related to psychological principles. For instance, heightened intuition might be a byproduct of advanced pattern recognition skills, often an attribute of emotional intelligence. Additionally, the placebo effect, a well-documented psychological phenomenon, may parallel the efficacy of certain psychic defense techniques. If an individual believes a specific amulet or ritual will protect them, the belief itself becomes a potent force, activating cognitive and emotional resources that can act as psychic armor.

Moreover, the concept of archetypes, introduced by Carl Jung, has direct implications in psychic phenomena. Archetypal symbols are powerful because they resonate with deeply ingrained cognitive patterns. Utilizing these symbols in rituals or visualizations can enhance the efficacy of psychic defense mechanisms. For example, the archetype of the "Warrior" can be summoned as a guardian entity during times of psychic vulnerability.

Emotional Management and Energy Fields

One of the cornerstone ideas of psychology is emotional regulation, the capability to influence and control emotional responses. In the context of psychic defense, emotional regulation is vital. Negative emotions like fear, anger, or anxiety can weaken one's psychic defenses, making one susceptible to psychic attacks. Techniques such as mindfulness meditation, often recommended in psychotherapy, can also serve as a powerful tool in managing the emotional states that interact with one's energy fields. By maintaining emotional equilibrium, you are less likely to attract negative energies or psychic attacks. Moreover, emotion-focused coping strategies can help in rapidly recovering from psychic disturbances, much in the same way they assist in overcoming psychological stressors.

Cognitive Restructuring: A Tool for Psychic Defense

Cognitive restructuring is a psychological technique aimed at identifying and challenging maladaptive thoughts and beliefs. This technique can also be applied to fortify psychic defenses. By reframing cognitive distortions like catastrophizing or black-and-white thinking, an individual can generate a psychic environment that is more resilient to external disruptions. For instance, if you hold the belief that you are perpetually vulnerable to psychic attacks, you may indeed attract those energies. Challenging and restructuring this belief can have a measurable impact on your psychic well-being.

In practice, cognitive restructuring can be combined with visualization techniques to create powerful psychic defense mechanisms. Imagine replacing a harmful thought pattern with a protective energy shield, seeing the old thought dissolve and the new protective shield solidify. The cognitive reframing fortifies the psychic protection mechanism, creating a recursive loop of positive psychic reinforcement.

This chapter has explored the intricate interconnections between psychology and psychic defense, examining how they can coexist and inform each other. Psychological constructs like emotional intelligence, archetypes, emotional regulation, and cognitive restructuring can be repurposed or integrated into psychic defense strategies. While psychology and psychic phenomena often inhabit different ontological spaces, the interstitial area between them is ripe for exploration. By merging the empirical with the esoteric, one can build a more robust, nuanced framework for psychic defense that draws strength from both realms. This blended approach can provide a fuller, more holistic way to safeguard one's psychic and emotional well-being, bridging the gap between the scientifically explainable and the as-yet unexplored mysteries of psychic phenomena.

CHAPTER 34:
EMERGING
TECHNOLOGIES AND
PSYCHIC DEFENSE

As we move into an era that blends age-old wisdom with cutting-edge technologies, the domain of psychic defense is not untouched by these advancements. While the underpinnings of energy fields, psychic phenomena, and defense mechanisms have remained mostly consistent through the millennia, there is a growing trend of incorporating technological tools to amplify or supplement traditional practices. This chapter aims to delve into some of these emerging technologies that are finding applications in psychic defense, from biofeedback systems to Virtual Reality (VR).

Biofeedback Systems and Psychic Defense

Biofeedback systems are a significant stride in the realm of healthcare and well-being. By translating physiological responses into real-time data, these systems enable an individual to gain insight into otherwise subconscious processes. Heart rate, skin conductance, and brainwave patterns are commonly measured parameters. How does this relate to psychic defense?

The crux of psychic defense is awareness—awareness of one's energy field, alterations in mood or physical state, and anomalies in the surrounding environment. Biofeedback can be an invaluable tool in gaining this awareness. For example, observing one's heart rate spike inexplicably might be an indication of a psychic attack or energy drain. Conversely, biofeedback can help an individual understand what a state of strong psychic defense looks like in terms of physiological metrics. In such scenarios, biofeedback acts as a compass, enabling a more responsive and tailored defense strategy. It offers a quantitative basis for something that is often seen as purely qualitative or even esoteric.

Virtual Reality (VR) and Augmented Reality (AR) for Immersive Training

The use of VR and AR in psychic defense is still in its infancy but holds promising potential. These technologies can be used to create simulated environments where an individual can practice psychic defense techniques in a safe, controlled setting.

Imagine, for instance, entering a virtual world designed to mimic situations that make you vulnerable to psychic attacks or energy drains. Within this world, you could practice grounding techniques, experiment with energy shields, or invoke spiritual allies, all while monitoring your physiological responses via biofeedback.

Incorporating VR and AR into training regimens allows for an immersive experience that could fast-track one's understanding and mastery of psychic defense. Moreover, these simulated environments can be shared across geographic locations, enabling collective training or even a form of networked psychic defense. Essentially, these technologies serve as a bridge between theoretical knowledge and practical application, while providing the added benefit of safety and repeatability.

Wearable Technology and Real-time Monitoring

Wearable technologies like smartwatches and fitness trackers have already made inroads into our daily lives, monitoring various aspects of our health. Advanced versions of these wearables are now coming equipped with more sensitive sensors capable of detecting subtle changes in our bio-energetic fields. Some are even equipped with environmental sensors that can detect changes in electromagnetic fields around us.

By setting up alerts and thresholds in such devices, one can be notified of potential psychic disturbances in real-time. These devices can even be synchronized with other systems, like smart home technologies, to create a fortified environment. For example, triggering calming music, dimming the lights, or even activating a pre-set aroma diffuser when the device senses heightened stress or other emotional disturbances, thereby contributing to strengthening psychic defenses.

The intersection of technology and psychic defense represents an evolving frontier that could significantly enhance the effectiveness and accessibility of psychic defense strategies. Biofeedback systems provide actionable, real-time data, helping to remove some of the ambiguity traditionally associated with psychic phenomena. VR and AR offer safe and controlled environments for practicing defense techniques, potentially accelerating the learning curve. Wearable technology brings real-time monitoring into the equation, providing an ongoing, dynamic layer of defense.

While the reliability and efficacy of these emerging technologies in the realm of psychic defense are still subjects of ongoing research and development, they offer intriguing possibilities. As with any tool, their effectiveness will depend on how they are utilized within the broader context of a well-rounded psychic defense strategy. It is essential to approach these technologies as complements to, rather than replacements for, traditional practices and techniques.

CHAPTER 35:
PREPARING FOR
UNUSUAL AND
EXTREME PSYCHIC
EVENTS

The realm of psychic defense often deals with everyday energies and potential psychic intrusions that many of us might encounter in normal life situations. However, there are rare and more extreme phenomena that, although unlikely, could pose a significant threat to your psychic integrity. These events can range from focused psychic attacks by skilled practitioners to cosmic or planetary shifts affecting the energy fields of individuals on a mass scale. This chapter will delve into strategies for navigating and defending against such extreme psychic events, including psychic "battles," mass energy shifts, and unexpected surges in psychic abilities.

Psychic Battles and Directed Attacks

The concept of a psychic "battle" may seem far-fetched or sensational, yet there are documented cases and traditions that speak of practitioners engaging in psychic duels, either for dominance, ideological differences, or as a test of skill. Preparation for such an extreme event involves a multi-layered strategy:

1. **Enhanced Shields:** Your regular psychic shielding techniques should be fortified. This could involve complex ritual work, specialized talismans, or invoking higher-level spiritual allies.

2. **Counter Techniques:** These are psychic maneuvers designed to reflect, absorb, or redirect incoming attacks. Examples include mirror shields that reflect energies back to the sender and psychic "traps" that can absorb and neutralize malicious intent.

3. **Offensive Measures:** Though the focus is on defense, sometimes a counter-attack is necessary to disable the opposing practitioner's ability to maintain their attack. This should be done with great care and ethical consideration.

Mass Energy Shifts

There are periods when large-scale energy shifts happen, often influenced by cosmic or astrological events. These aren't targeted attacks but can still wreak havoc on your psychic defenses. Preparing for these events often involves:

1. **Awareness:** Keep yourself updated on astrological forecasts or cosmic events that are expected to result in energy shifts. Knowledge is power.

2. **Adaptive Shielding:** Create flexible and adaptive psychic shields that can more readily adjust to varying types of energy. This might include visualizations that involve fluid-like barriers rather than rigid ones.

3. **Group Work:** Sometimes collective energy can help offset destabilizing influences. Participate in group rituals or collective meditations designed to stabilize the energy field around you and your community.

Unexpected Surges in Psychic Abilities

Some individuals experience sudden and intense "awakenings," where their psychic abilities ramp up dramatically over a short period. While this can be exciting, it can also be disorienting and make you more susceptible to psychic phenomena, both positive and negative. In these situations:

1. **Grounding:** Extra grounding work can help manage the increased sensitivity.

2. **Mentorship:** Seek guidance from more experienced practitioners who can provide personalized advice.

3. **Temporary Isolation:** Minimize exposure to stimuli that could trigger overwhelming psychic experiences. This is not a long-term strategy but can provide short-term relief as you adjust.

These are extraordinary circumstances that call for a blending of advanced psychic defense techniques, often used in combination for the most effective protection. The development of one's skills to meet these challenges often involves committed practice, specialized knowledge, and sometimes mentorship or guidance from those who have navigated similar challenges.

While most individuals exploring psychic defense will likely never face these extreme events, being prepared for them can offer insights into the deeper layers of psychic defense and the potentials of human consciousness. These advanced strategies not only serve as preparations for rare psychic challenges but can also strengthen your everyday psychic defense mechanisms. They push the boundaries of what we understand as psychic phenomena and defense, offering a glimpse into the complexity and depth of the energetic universe.

CHAPTER 36:
CONCLUSION:
BUILDING A
PERSONALIZED
PSYCHIC DEFENSE
STRATEGY

As we close this comprehensive guide on psychic defense, the focus turns to integrating all the knowledge and tools amassed to build a personalized strategy that resonates with you. Given the spectrum of psychic phenomena and defense techniques explored, it is only fitting that your approach to psychic protection be equally nuanced, adaptable, and multi-layered.

Assessing Your Psychic Landscape

The first step in building a personalized psychic defense strategy involves an honest self-assessment. By now, you should be familiar with the symptoms and sources of psychic attacks, different types of energy fields, and how various psychic phenomena operate. This foundational knowledge allows you to evaluate your susceptibility to certain types of psychic interactions.

For example, if you are more prone to experiencing psychic "static" when engaging in social media, your focus could be on digital spaces defense. Alternatively, if you find that you are sensitive to collective energies, then methods for defense against collective psychic phenomena would be crucial for you. A self-assessment helps you prioritize the techniques that are most relevant to your lifestyle and psychic vulnerabilities.

Tailoring Techniques and Tools

Once you have an understanding of your own psychic landscape, the next step is to choose defense mechanisms that align with your needs. Techniques range from basic, such as grounding and shielding, to more advanced tactics like invoking spiritual allies or astral defense. Tools can also be integrated into your strategy. Whether you resonate more with crystals, rituals, or sacred geometry, your choice of tools should serve to empower your chosen techniques.

Remember that the utility of a tool or technique is subjective.

Just because a specific crystal is universally acclaimed for its protective properties does not mean it will work for you in the same way. Experiment with different tools and techniques, keeping track of the results to fine-tune your approach. Moreover, pay attention to the ethical considerations discussed earlier; your defenses should not become a means to infringe upon others' energetic spaces or free will.

The Importance of Adaptive Strategy

The psychic realm, much like the physical world, is in constant flux. What worked yesterday may not be effective tomorrow. Therefore, it's essential to approach your psychic defense strategy as a living, evolving entity. Regular reassessments are critical for ensuring that your defenses evolve alongside your psychic landscape. This might mean introducing new techniques, phasing out outdated ones, or even reconsidering the ethical implications of your strategy as you grow in psychic understanding.

Furthermore, embrace the technological innovations mentioned in previous chapters, such as biofeedback or virtual reality, which offer new avenues for psychic defense. New modalities can integrate seamlessly with traditional approaches, thus enriching your defense toolkit.

Building a personalized psychic defense strategy requires ongoing engagement with both external phenomena and internal sensitivities. Your strategy should be founded upon a keen understanding of your psychic vulnerabilities, enriched by carefully chosen techniques and tools, and remain open to evolution as you continue to navigate the psychic realm. Just as there is no one-size-fits-all approach to psychic phenomena, there is no ultimate, immutable strategy for psychic defense. Your personalized plan should be as unique, dynamic, and multi-faceted as the psychic world it serves to navigate and protect. And with that, you are now better equipped to safeguard your energetic well-being in a world teeming with both magical opportunities and psychic challenges.

APPENDIX A: EASTERN VERSUS WESTERN APPROACHES TO PSYCHIC DEFENSE

The approaches to psychic defense in Eastern and Western traditions reflect deeper philosophical underpinnings and cultural values that influence how psychic phenomena are understood and managed.

Eastern Approaches:

Eastern traditions, particularly those from Asian cultures, emphasize the interconnectedness of all things and the cultivation of personal energy as a way to achieve psychological and spiritual well-being. Practices such as meditation, yoga, and Tai Chi are integral, focusing on the flow and balance of energy within the body and the universe. These practices often aim to help individuals understand and dissolve the ego, which is seen not as a central identity to be strengthened, but as an illusion to be transcended.

In Eastern psychology, there is a focus on inner development and the awareness of one's place within the larger cosmos. This inward focus is aimed at achieving a state of enlightenment or awakening, where the individual perceives themselves as part of an interconnected whole, leading to enhanced well-being and reduced psychological suffering. The therapeutic aspect of Eastern practices is rooted in everyday living, aiding individuals to function optimally within their environments and relationships through a profound understanding of self and other as interconnected.

Western Approaches:

Western approaches, by contrast, often employ methodologies that are more analytical and focused on the individual as a separate entity. Western psychology typically engages in practices that treat psychological symptoms through distinct methodologies like psychotherapy and counseling, which are oriented towards changing or managing one's consciousness and behavioral outcomes.

In psychic defense, Western traditions might focus more on the protection of the individual's psychic space through shielding techniques, use of crystals, and invoking protective spirits or entities. There is a significant emphasis on setting boundaries and actively guarding against external psychic influences. Western methods are more likely to incorporate tools and rituals that can be observed and measured, reflecting a broader cultural tendency towards empiricism and the material aspects of psychic phenomena.

Integrative Practices:

Interestingly, there has been a growing integration of Eastern methodologies within Western practices as the benefits of holistic and preventive care are increasingly recognized in psychological health. Practices like mindfulness and meditation have been incorporated into Western therapeutic practices, showing effectiveness in enhancing mental resilience and reducing symptoms of various psychological conditions. This integration reflects a shift towards a more holistic view of psychic defense, acknowledging the value of both external protections and internal resilience.

Both Eastern and Western approaches offer valuable insights and techniques for psychic defense. While Eastern methods emphasize understanding and integrating internal processes for comprehensive psychic resilience, Western practices focus on actionable defenses against external threats. The integration of these philosophies offers a more complete toolkit for individuals seeking to protect their psychic space in a complex world.

Indigenous and Shamanic Practices

Indigenous and shamanic traditions from various cultures around the world offer unique insights and methods for psychic defense, reflecting a deep connection with nature, ancestral wisdom, and the spiritual realm. These practices, often passed down through generations, emphasize the harmony between humans and the natural world and provide a rich tapestry of techniques for protecting and cleansing the psychic self.

Indigenous Practices:

Indigenous psychic defense practices are deeply woven with the cultural fabric of a community, often centered around the belief in the spiritual potency of natural elements and ancestral guidance. For example, Native American traditions frequently incorporate the use of smudging with sage, cedar, or sweetgrass to cleanse a space or individual from negative energy. These practices are not just about removing unwanted energies but also about restoring balance and harmony within the individual and their environment.

In the shamanic traditions of the Amazon, practitioners—often called shamans—use a combination of rituals, herbal medicines, and spirit consultations to diagnose and heal psychic disturbances. These shamans act as mediators between the physical world and the spirit world, navigating these realms through altered states of consciousness induced by rhythmic drumming, chanting, or the use of entheogens like ayahuasca. The belief here is that psychic ailments are often manifestations of spiritual or emotional imbalances that require holistic healing approaches.

Shamanic Practices Across the Globe:

Shamanic practices extend beyond the Amazon and are found in cultures from Siberia to Indonesia. In Siberian shamanism, the concept of psychic defense might involve the shaman entering a trance state to combat or negotiate with malevolent spirits believed to cause illness or misfortune. The shaman's tools— drums, rattles, and sometimes elaborate costumes—serve both as symbolic armor and as instruments to facilitate these spiritual journeys.

In parts of Asia, such as Mongolia and Korea, shamans perform elaborate rituals that often serve to protect individuals, families, or entire communities from psychic harm. These rituals can include dance, music, and the creation of protective talismans. The underlying belief is that by appeasing or controlling spiritual forces, one can maintain not just physical and mental health but also psychic integrity.

Commonalities and Differences:

Despite the geographical and cultural diversity among indigenous and shamanic practices, common themes emerge, such as the importance of the natural world, the use of ritual, and the belief in a permeable boundary between the spiritual and physical worlds. These practices highlight a form of psychic defense that is dynamic and interactive, contrasting with more static methods such as the use of fixed talismans or shields common in Western psychic defense strategies.

The emphasis in many indigenous and shamanic practices is not only on protection but also on the restoration of balance and harmony within the individual and their community. This holistic approach views psychic defense as a part of a broader spiritual health regimen, integrating the individual's well-being with that of their community and environment.

Indigenous and shamanic approaches to psychic defense provide a rich, varied perspective that complements the more individualistic and material-focused methods often found in Western practices. These traditions teach us that psychic defense can be a deeply spiritual practice that encompasses not just the individual but also their relationship with the wider world.

APPENDIX B: PARAPSYCHOLOGY RESEARCH

The field of parapsychology, which studies psychic phenomena such as extrasensory perception (ESP), telepathy, and psychokinesis, exists in a unique scientific and scholarly niche. Despite facing significant skepticism and criticism from the mainstream scientific community, dedicated research institutions and foundations have been committed to investigating these phenomena under rigorous experimental conditions.

Research Foundations and Contributions:

Organizations like the Alex Tanous Foundation for Scientific Research have amassed decades of research on psychic phenomena, aiming to explore these phenomena through a scientific lens. The foundation focuses not only on collecting and preserving past research but also on encouraging new studies and discussions in the field, thus supporting a deeper understanding and validation of psychic experiences.

Similarly, the Society for Psychical Research in London and the Parapsychology Foundation have played pivotal roles in providing a platform for the scientific investigation of psychic phenomena. These institutions help bridge the gap between paranormal experiences and scientific inquiry by publishing research findings, hosting conferences, and educating the public and academics alike.

Experimental Methods and Studies:

One of the notable methodologies in parapsychology research is the ganzfeld experiment, a technique designed to test individuals for telepathic abilities. This method involves placing a receiver in a sensory-reduced environment to see if they can receive mental information from a sender located in a different place. Such experiments have occasionally produced results that suggest a higher-than-chance rate of information transfer, hinting at the potential for telepathic communication.

Remote viewing is another area of interest in parapsychology. This practice involves participants trying to describe or draw detailed information about a location or object that is hidden from their physical view, sometimes at a great distance. This form of ESP has been explored both by independent researchers and, historically, in programs funded by government agencies, which sought to evaluate its potential for intelligence gathering.

Challenges and Skepticism:

Despite these intriguing findings, parapsychology is often labeled as a pseudoscience by mainstream scientists. This criticism stems from the difficulties in replicating the results reliably and the lack of a clear mechanism to explain how psychic phenomena could occur within the known laws of physics. As a result, most studies on psychic phenomena are published in specialized journals rather than mainstream scientific outlets.

The field of parapsychology embodies a significant tension between open-minded exploration and the rigorous skepticism required by the scientific method. While there are documented instances and experimental data that suggest the existence of psychic phenomena, the broader scientific community remains cautious, emphasizing the need for more reliable and consistent evidence to shift the prevailing views on these contentious topics.

The scientific investigation of psychic phenomena continues to be a challenging field, marked by both fascination and skepticism. Research efforts from dedicated foundations and ongoing experiments like those involving the ganzfeld technique and remote viewing contribute to a complex but intriguing picture of human capabilities beyond conventional sensory experiences.

Critiques and Controversies in Parapsychology

The field of parapsychology, which explores phenomena such as telepathy, clairvoyance, and psychokinesis, has been the subject of considerable debate and skepticism within the broader scientific community. This skepticism is rooted in various challenges related to methodological rigor, the reproducibility of results, and the theoretical foundations of the discipline.

Scientific and Philosophical Skepticism:

A significant portion of the scientific community remains skeptical of parapsychology, critiquing it for a perceived lack of adherence to the conventional scientific method and the difficulty in replicating its experimental results. Critics argue that parapsychological studies often fail to eliminate all possible natural explanations for observed effects, which casts doubt on the validity of their findings. Furthermore, the theoretical mechanisms proposed to explain psychic phenomena are often seen as incompatible with established principles of physics and biology, contributing to its marginalization from mainstream science.

Methodological Challenges:

Parapsychology's methodologies have been a particular point of contention. Critics point out that studies in parapsychology sometimes suffer from methodological flaws such as inadequate controls, small sample sizes, and statistical errors. These issues can lead to false positives or the misinterpretation of data. Additionally, there is the problem of the "file drawer" effect, where only studies with positive results are published, while negative outcomes remain unpublished, skewing the overall scientific literature towards seemingly supportive findings.

Institutional and Cultural Biases:

The dismissal of parapsychology can also be attributed to broader cultural and institutional biases. Historical biases rooted in colonialist and materialist perspectives have shaped scientific discourse, leading to a privileging of certain types of knowledge and methodologies over others. This has often resulted in a systemic marginalization of fields like parapsychology, which challenge conventional scientific paradigms.

The Role of Skepticism and Dialogue:

Despite these challenges, the field of parapsychology continues to evolve, with proponents advocating for more rigorous methodologies and openness to skeptical scrutiny. Institutions like the Parapsychological Association emphasize the importance of critical feedback and collaboration between skeptics and proponents to enhance the robustness of research methods. Such dialogues are crucial for advancing scientific understanding and integrating parapsychological research with broader scientific efforts.

While parapsychology faces significant challenges and skepticism, it also represents a dynamic area of study that continues to push the boundaries of our understanding of consciousness and human capabilities. Ongoing efforts to refine its methodologies and engage in open, critical dialogue are vital for its future development and potential integration into the mainstream scientific landscape.

APPENDIX C: LEGAL FRAMEWORKS GOVERNING PSYCHIC PRACTICES

The regulation of psychic practices, encompassing activities such as psychic readings, spiritual healing, and the sale of metaphysical goods, varies significantly across different jurisdictions. The legal frameworks governing these practices often balance consumer protection with religious and cultural freedoms, resulting in a complex mosaic of laws and regulations.

Constitutional and Statutory Provisions:

In many countries, psychic practices are indirectly influenced by constitutional rights, such as the freedom of religion and belief. For instance, spiritual and psychic practices might be protected under broader religious practices, which are constitutionally safeguarded in many democratic societies. However, these practices also fall under general consumer protection laws designed to prevent fraud and ensure the fairness of commercial transactions. These laws regulate claims made by practitioners about the efficacy or outcomes of their services, which must not mislead consumers.

Specific Legal Regulations and Guidelines:

Some regions have specific statutes or guidelines directly addressing psychic practices. For example, in certain states or countries, there are explicit requirements for the disclaimers that psychics must provide to clients, stipulating that such services are for entertainment purposes only. Additionally, local business licensing requirements might apply, where psychics must obtain a permit to operate legally. These local regulations are primarily aimed at consumer protection, ensuring that clients are not misled or defrauded.

Challenges in Legal Enforcement:

Enforcing these laws can be challenging due to the subjective and personal nature of psychic services. The effectiveness or authenticity of psychic readings and spiritual healing is difficult to prove or disprove, complicating regulatory efforts. Legal systems must navigate the fine line between protecting consumers and infringing on personal beliefs and religious freedoms. The variability in how psychic practices are perceived culturally and legally also affects the consistency of enforcement across different regions.

Emerging Trends and Legal Adaptations:

The legal landscape is continuously adapting to new developments in the field of psychic practices, especially with the rise of digital platforms offering psychic services. Online psychic readings and spiritual counseling present new challenges for regulation and consumer protection, prompting lawmakers and regulators to update existing frameworks to accommodate these modern changes. This includes adapting laws that govern remote commercial transactions and digital consumer interactions.

The legal frameworks governing psychic practices demonstrate the complex interplay between consumer protection laws and the protection of religious and cultural practices. As the practice of psychic services evolves, especially with technological advancements, legal systems worldwide are challenged to adapt and provide clear, enforceable guidelines that safeguard both practitioners and consumers without compromising cultural and spiritual expressions.

Ethical Guidelines for Psychic Defense Practitioners

Ethical guidelines play a crucial role in governing the practices of those involved in psychic defense. These guidelines help ensure that practitioners act responsibly, respect the rights of their clients, and promote integrity and transparency in their practices. Establishing a strong ethical framework is essential for maintaining public trust and professional credibility in the field of psychic defense.

Principle of Non-Maleficence:

One of the foundational ethical principles in psychic defense is non-maleficence, which is the commitment to do no harm. Practitioners must ensure that their interventions do not cause physical, psychological, or spiritual harm to their clients. This includes being mindful of the client's emotional and mental state and refraining from exploiting their vulnerabilities for financial or personal gain. Psychic defense should be aimed at empowering and protecting the client, rather than creating dependency or fear.

Informed Consent and Confidentiality:

Practitioners are ethically obliged to obtain informed consent from their clients before commencing any psychic defense work. This involves clearly explaining the nature of the services, potential risks, and expected outcomes. Clients should feel free to ask questions and withdraw consent at any point if they feel uncomfortable with the process. Alongside informed consent, maintaining confidentiality is paramount. Information shared by clients during sessions should be kept confidential unless explicit permission is given to share specific details for a relevant purpose.

Professional Boundaries:

Maintaining professional boundaries is crucial in psychic defense practices. Practitioners must avoid dual relationships that can lead to conflicts of interest or exploitation. This includes personal, sexual, or financial relationships that might impair their professional judgment or harm the client. Setting clear boundaries helps in preserving the integrity of the practitioner-client relationship and ensures that the focus remains on the client's welfare.

Accuracy and Honesty:

Practitioners should always communicate honestly with their clients about what psychic defense can and cannot do. They should avoid making exaggerated claims about their abilities or the effectiveness of their techniques. It is important to provide a realistic assessment of the situation and to manage expectations. Practitioners should also recognize the limits of their skills and refer clients to other professionals when necessary, such as licensed therapists or medical doctors, if their needs go beyond what psychic defense can provide.

Cultural Sensitivity and Respect:

Given the diverse backgrounds from which clients may come,

practitioners must demonstrate cultural sensitivity and respect for different beliefs and practices. Psychic defense should not impose one cultural perspective over another but rather should adapt and respect the cultural context of the client. This includes being aware of cultural specifics that might influence the client's understanding and experience of psychic phenomena and defense strategies.

Ethical guidelines are essential for guiding the practice of psychic defense, ensuring that it is conducted responsibly and with the highest regard for the welfare of the client. These principles help safeguard both the practitioner and the client, fostering a trusting and professional relationship that is conducive to effective psychic defense. Adhering to these ethical standards helps elevate the field and ensures that it is recognized as a legitimate and respected practice.

APPENDIX D: TALISMANS AND AMULETS

Talismans and amulets have been integral to psychic defense across various cultures and historical periods, serving as protective tools against negative energies or psychic attacks. Understanding their uses, materials, and methods of consecration can provide invaluable insights into their enduring role in spiritual practices.

Historical Significance and Usage:

Talismans and amulets are often used interchangeably but serve slightly different purposes. Amulets are typically worn for general protection and to ward off evil, while talismans are usually crafted to draw specific energies or to enhance certain aspects of the wearer's life. Historically, these objects have been used in many cultures—from the ancient Egyptians and Romans to medieval Europe and indigenous tribes worldwide. They were, and in many cultures still are, believed to possess properties that protect the wearer from harm or bring good fortune.

Materials and Craftsmanship:

The materials used in making talismans and amulets are as varied as the cultures they come from. Common materials include herbs, stones, crystals, metals, bones, and woods. Each material is often chosen for its specific metaphysical properties. For example, iron is traditionally used in fairy folklore for its protective properties against malevolent spirits, while turquoise is prized in Native American culture for its healing and protective qualities.

Craftsmanship is also a critical aspect, as many traditions hold that the manner in which a talisman or amulet is made contributes to its effectiveness. The creation of these objects often involves rituals or prayers, which are said to charge the items with protective energy. This process may be governed by astrological conditions or specific spiritual or religious guidelines, enhancing the talisman or amulet's perceived potency.

Methods of Consecration:

Consecration is a critical step in preparing talismans and amulets for use. This process involves blessing or imbuing them with spiritual power, which can be performed through various rituals depending on cultural or individual practices. For instance, some might be consecrated in a ritual that includes elements like fire, water, earth, and air to align the item with natural forces. Others might be prayed over by a spiritual leader or anointed with oils that are believed to carry psychic protective properties.

In some traditions, the timing of the creation and consecration of talismans and amulets is also crucial. For example, some practitioners prefer to work during specific lunar phases or planetary hours, which are believed to enhance the effectiveness of the talisman or amulet in accordance with astrological beliefs.

Cultural Variations and Modern Adaptations:

While the basic concept of talismans and amulets is similar across different cultures, their designs, interpretations, and uses vary significantly. In contemporary times, these objects have seen a resurgence in popularity not only among those who follow traditional spiritual paths but also among people looking for personal empowerment or protection in their daily lives.

Today, talismans and amulets are not only part of spiritual practice but have also been adapted by modern jewelry and fashion industries, merging aesthetic appeal with spiritual significance. This blend of tradition and modernity ensures that the ancient practice of using talismans and amulets continues to evolve and remain relevant in contemporary society.

Talismans and amulets serve as fascinating examples of the intersection between cultural tradition, craftsmanship, and spiritual belief, offering both historical context and a practical application in psychic defense practices. Their continued use highlights the universal human desire for protection and the influence of spiritual or mystical beliefs in human life.

Sacred Texts and Mantras

Sacred texts and mantras are pivotal components of spiritual traditions worldwide, playing a crucial role in psychic defense by fostering spiritual protection and mental resilience. These spiritual tools are employed across various cultures to shield individuals from negative influences and enhance spiritual awareness.

Role of Sacred Texts in Psychic Defense:

Sacred texts, such as the Bible, Quran, Bhagavad Gita, and many others, are often used as sources of psychic protection. They provide guidelines, stories, and prayers that many believe to contain protective powers. In some traditions, specific verses or chapters are recited as a means of safeguarding against psychic attacks or negative energies. For instance, Psalm 91 in the Christian Bible is frequently recited for protection in times of danger.

These texts often serve as moral and ethical guides, strengthening the practitioner's spiritual foundation and providing a source of comfort and resilience against psychic disturbances. The act of reading or reciting these texts can also be a meditative practice, helping to center the mind, fortify the spirit, and align the individual with divine protection.

Power and Use of Mantras:

Mantras are sacred phrases, sounds, or syllables that are believed to have psychological and spiritual powers. Originating from Hinduism and Buddhism, mantras are now integral to many spiritual practices around the world. They are thought to transform consciousness, purify the mind, and protect against psychic disturbances.

Each mantra has a specific vibration and meaning, which is said to manifest spiritual energy when vocalized or chanted. For example, the "Om Mani Padme Hum" mantra in Tibetan Buddhism is used to invoke the benevolent and protective attention of Chenrezig, the embodiment of compassion. Similarly, the "Gayatri Mantra" is widely used in Hinduism for its protective and enlightening properties.

Integrating Mantras and Sacred Texts in Daily Practice:

Incorporating sacred texts and mantras into daily life can involve ritualistic reading, recitation, or chanting, often at specific times of the day or in particular circumstances. Many practitioners choose to begin their day with a reading or recitation, setting a protected and positive tone for the day ahead.

The use of these texts and mantras can also be situational, employed specifically when facing challenging or threatening situations where psychic defense is deemed necessary. Some individuals carry physical copies of sacred texts or inscriptions of mantras with them as talismans for continuous protection.

Cultural and Personal Adaptations:

While the use of sacred texts and mantras is deeply rooted in specific religious and cultural practices, individuals often adapt these to their personal needs and understandings. This adaptability allows people from various spiritual backgrounds to find and use texts and mantras in ways that resonate personally and effectively for psychic defense.

In essence, sacred texts and mantras provide more than just spiritual knowledge—they are active tools in psychic defense, offering both protective energy and a means to deepen one's spiritual practice. Whether used for regular meditation, in response to specific threats, or as a preventive measure, these spiritual resources help individuals maintain psychic integrity and spiritual health.

APPENDIX E: HOLISTIC HEALTH PRACTICES

Holistic health practices, which emphasize the integration of physical, mental, and spiritual well-being, play a crucial role in psychic defense. These practices, including yoga, Tai Chi, and Qigong, not only enhance physical health but also bolster psychic resilience, providing a strong defense against negative energies and psychic disturbances.

Yoga: Integration of Body, Mind, and Spirit

Yoga, an ancient practice originating from India, incorporates physical postures (asanas), meditation, and breath control (pranayama) to enhance overall well-being. In the context of psychic defense, yoga serves as a powerful tool for grounding and centering the practitioner, aligning the physical and energetic bodies, and strengthening the aura against external psychic influences.

The regular practice of yoga helps in maintaining a balanced energy flow throughout the body, which is essential for shielding oneself against psychic attacks. Certain yoga poses are particularly effective for grounding, such as Tadasana (Mountain Pose) and Balasana (Child's Pose), which help stabilize the practitioner's energy and connect them more deeply with the earth.

Tai Chi: The Art of Flowing Energy

Tai Chi, a martial art from China known for its slow and graceful movements, is another holistic practice that enhances psychic defense. It is often described as meditation in motion, promoting deep relaxation and inner peace. Tai Chi improves the flow of Qi (vital energy) throughout the body, fortifying the practitioner's energy field and creating a barrier against harmful external influences.

The continuous, flowing movements of Tai Chi help to dissolve energy blockages and promote an equilibrium that is both physically and psychically protective. Regular practice can increase mental clarity and awareness, enabling practitioners to detect and neutralize negative energies before they become disruptive.

Qigong: Cultivating Energy for Health and Defense

Qigong, similar to Tai Chi, involves rhythmic movements, focused breathing, and intentional visualization to enhance life energy. This practice is particularly effective in building and maintaining a vibrant, resilient energy field, which acts as a natural defense mechanism against psychic disturbances.

One of the key aspects of Qigong in psychic defense is its emphasis on energy cultivation and management. Through various Qigong exercises, practitioners learn to control and direct their Qi, using it to cleanse, strengthen, and protect their aura. This capability is crucial in managing the psychic environment, allowing for the clearing of negative energies and the reinforcement of positive, protective energies.

Integrating Practices into Daily Life

Integrating these holistic health practices into daily life can significantly enhance an individual's psychic defenses. Regular engagement with yoga, Tai Chi, or Qigong not only improves physical health but also builds spiritual resilience and psychic protection. These practices can be tailored to fit the needs and lifestyles of individuals, whether through classes, personal practice, or even short daily sessions.

Holistic health practices such as yoga, Tai Chi, and Qigong play a vital role in psychic defense. By enhancing physical health, promoting energy balance, and strengthening the psychic field, these practices provide individuals with the tools needed to maintain both physical and psychic integrity in the face of various psychic challenges.

Bioenergetic Exercises

Bioenergetic exercises, a series of physical activities designed to enhance the body's energy flow and emotional balance, play a crucial role in maintaining and protecting one's energy field. These exercises are based on the principles of bioenergetics, which combine physical movement, breathwork, and emotional expression to release stress, improve health, and strengthen psychic defenses.

Understanding Bioenergetics:

Bioenergetics is rooted in the understanding that the body and mind are interconnected, and that emotional or psychological distress can manifest as physical tension. This concept is central to many holistic health practices, which aim to address both mental and physical aspects simultaneously. Bioenergetic exercises are designed to help individuals resolve emotional issues through active and expressive body movements, thereby clearing and strengthening their energy fields.

Key Bioenergetic Exercises:

1. **Grounding Exercises:**
   - Grounding exercises focus on establishing a strong connection with the earth, which is essential for stability and energy flow. These exercises often involve standing positions where the feet are firmly planted on the ground, helping to cultivate a sense of security and physical connection to the earth. This grounding is believed to enhance one's ability to manage external psychic influences.

2. **Breathing Techniques:**
   - Proper breathing is fundamental in bioenergetics, as it is thought to influence the flow of Qi, or vital energy, throughout the body. Deep, diaphragmatic breathing is encouraged to help release energy blockages and promote relaxation. Techniques may include breathing through emotional tension and focusing on the expansion and contraction of the abdomen to increase awareness of bodily sensations.

3. **Stress Release Exercises:**
   - These involve physical activities that encourage the release of built-up tension. Activities might include punching or kicking into the air, screaming, or other forms of cathartic expression. Such exercises are not only liberating but also beneficial for breaking through emotional barriers, which can fortify psychic defenses by reducing vulnerability to negative energies.

4. **Character Stances:**

- Developed from Wilhelm Reich's character analysis, these stances involve adopting body positions that correlate with certain personality types or emotional states. Each stance is designed to confront and modify specific emotional conflicts, helping individuals overcome psychic and emotional blockages that could make them susceptible to psychic disturbances.

Integrating Bioenergetic Exercises into Psychic Defense:

Incorporating bioenergetic exercises into a regular wellness routine can significantly enhance one's psychic defense by aligning and strengthening the body's energy field. Practitioners often report increased emotional resilience and a heightened sense of well-being, which contribute to stronger psychic boundaries.

For those involved in psychic defense, these exercises provide a practical tool for maintaining energy hygiene. Regular practice helps in managing sensitivity to external energies and supports overall emotional and physical health, creating a robust foundation for psychic integrity.

Bioenergetic exercises offer a dynamic approach to enhancing psychic defense through the integration of physical health and emotional well-being. By focusing on body awareness, emotional release, and energy flow, these exercises not only improve physical vitality but also contribute to a more resilient and protective psychic environment. For anyone engaged in psychic practices, bioenergetic exercises can be an essential part of maintaining balance and strength in both the physical and psychic realms.

THE END

Made in United States
North Haven, CT
28 July 2024

55537494R00098